The Complete Book of Vegan Compleating

An A–Z of zero-waste eating
for the mindful vegan

Ellen Tout

The Complete Book of Vegan Compleating
Ellen Tout

First published in the UK and USA in 2021 by
Nourish, an imprint of Watkins Media Limited
Unit 11, Shepperton House
83–93 Shepperton Road
London N1 3DF

enquiries@watkinspublishing.com

Commissioning Editor: Ella Chappell
Managing Editor: Daniel Culver
Interior Design: Luise Roberts
Illustrations: Liz Child
Production: Uzma Taj

Typeset in Archer
Printed in the United Kingdom by TJ Books Ltd

A CIP record for this book is available from the
British Library

ISBN: 978-1-84899-394-5 (Paperback)

10 9 8 7 6 5 4 3 2 1

Publisher's note
While every care has been taken in compiling
the recipes for this book, Watkins Media
Limited, or any other persons who have been
involved in working on this publication,
cannot accept responsibility for any errors
or omissions, inadvertent or not, that may
be found in the recipes or text, nor for
any problems that may arise as a result of
preparing one of these recipes. Ill or elderly
people, babies, young children, people who are
pregnant or breastfeeding/chestfeeding, or
anyone with any special dietary requirements
or medical conditions, are advised to consult
a medical professional before following any of
the recipes contained in this book.

Notes on the recipes
Unless otherwise stated:
• Use free-range eggs and poultry
• Use medium eggs, fruit and vegetables
• Use fresh ingredients, including herbs and
chillies
• Do not mix metric and imperial
measurements:
   1 tsp = 5ml   1 tbsp = 15ml   1 cup = 250ml

*For all the fellow waste
warriors and creative
plant-based cooks.*

*Thank you to Nadia for all
the support, cups of tea,
slices of banana bread, and
for helping taste-test every
recipe in this book.*

Contents

Key to Compleating

The icons throughout this book show which parts of different produce can be used, such as peels, cores or seeds. I've also included ways to upcycle, repurpose, reuse or grow from the parts you might usually throw away.

 Flesh

 Skin

 Core

 Stalk

 Whole spear

 Odds and ends

 Juices / liquid

 Beans

 Flowers

 Seeds

 Leaves / tops

 Roots

 Household and upcycling ideas

 How to ...

 Green-fingered Ideas

 Compleat

 Green pet foods

Use this key to quickly reference the part or tip you're looking for.

Introduction

"You cannot get through a single day without having an impact on the world around you. What you do makes a difference, and you have to decide what kind of difference you want to make." – Dr Jane Goodall

Why compleat?

It all started with a pumpkin one Halloween. As it sat on our kitchen worktop, ready for carving, I couldn't help but question if it was destined for more. With its beautiful orange skin, sweet autumnal flesh and abundance of seeds – maybe this year we should cook it instead? And so began an afternoon of cooking, and a new yearly tradition. From one pumpkin, we created soup, curry and pie, as well as treats for my dog. I looked at the mass of seeds and peelings and wondered if we could eat those too. Within minutes we were munching on delicious smoky roasted pumpkin crisps and seeds.

To "compleat" means to eat all edible parts of fruits, vegetables and herbs. The more I experimented, the more I discovered. It turns out that compleating is rather moreish! It was as if I was relearning how to cook. What can you do with leftover vegetable peelings? Do you have to trim the top off a leek? Why don't we use the whole chilli or ginger root? And why do we hardly ever see, let alone eat, the beautiful leafy tops from root vegetables? Often the "rules" about cooking and food preparation are habits learned from our parents or from recipe books, so we don't think to question why we discard some parts and eat others.

Growing up, my parents always used the old adage of "waste not, want not". We don't have to look back too far to find that some of the recipe ideas in this book are not new – we have just forgotten them. Many of our grandparents would have cooked with every single part of their ingredients. Offcuts from produce might have been simmered into stock, leftover lemon skins were often used for cleaning, and many more people grew, harvested and preserved their own produce. My nan always had jars of homemade pickles stored in her kitchen cupboards. If we look back to wartime Britain, people made the most of ingredients, cooking with things like the stalks from cauliflowers, the tops from beetroots, turnips and carrots, and the pods from peas and beans. Carrot cake and, one of my favourites, carrot top soup, are both recipes from that era.

I believe that today, many of us have lost that connection with nature and where our food comes from – the magic of sowing a seed, seeing the plant flourish and making the most of its whole harvest. We're so used to finding produce pre-prepared, packaged and trimmed, but it can be so much fun to rediscover ingredients and rethink how we cook with them.

There are so many reasons to compleat. Compleating is environmental, ethical, nourishing, creative, delicious, rewarding, and saves you money – it just makes good sense! Sadly, in the UK, 70 per cent of the food waste from our homes could have been eaten![1] When food reaches landfill, it can't compost naturally and can take many years to degrade, releasing methane in the process. This is responsible for eight per cent of global greenhouse gases. On top of that, there's also the land, energy, water, transport and resources involved in producing the food to begin with. Of course, composting uneaten food is a better option than sending it to landfill, but isn't cooking with it an even better, and way more exciting, one? Compleating is cooking good food, from all possible parts of the ingredient.

Often the peels, seeds and offcuts we commonly discard are actually brimming with flavour and nutrients. Seeds, like those from a melon, squash or pumpkin, are filled with the energy and goodness that the plant needs to sprout, grow and fruit. The skin, on the other hand, is crammed with everything the plant uses to protect itself, plus extra fibre and nutrition. The leafy tops from root vegetables are also packed with

1 *Food surplus and waste in the UK* – key facts report, WRAP, 2020.

vitamins and minerals, just like other greens that we do eat. Cooking with these parts introduces more colour and variety into your diet, as well as extra vitamins, minerals and natural goodness. When eating the whole ingredient, I do recommend that you scrub your produce well and choose organic if you can.

When my fascination with compleating first began, I searched everywhere for a book about reducing food waste for vegans. I found hundreds of books that included tips for cooking with leftover or offcut meat or dairy but not a single one dedicated to fruits, vegetables and herbs. That planted the seed of an idea that continued to grow: *The Complete Book of Vegan Compleating*. This is a book for anyone who wants to make the most of plant-based ingredients, whether you're vegan or not. Be it a glut of courgettes/zucchini grown at your allotment, a pile of skins from cooking onions or the peels from your daily banana, I truly hope that this book helps inspire you to cook with more variety and imagination and less waste.

About me

I have been vegetarian since childhood and chose to be vegan as an adult for ethical and environmental reasons. I am a freelance journalist and writer, specializing in sustainability and wellbeing. For the last few years, I have worked as the Eco Living Editor for *Psychologies* magazine, where I also wrote a monthly "Eco Worrier" column. As a journalist, I see my writing as a tool for good and choose to write about things that really matter and make a positive difference.

I live in Kent with my girlfriend and rescue bulldog Bella. When I'm not writing, you'll find me walking on the beach, climbing mountains and cooking or growing vegan food. I am passionate about protecting our oceans and the environment and finding practical ways for us all to be kinder to the planet. I also volunteer as a Coastal Guardian with Kent Wildlife Trust and with my local Friends of the Earth group.

During the process of writing this book, I have felt aware that I am not a chef – just someone with a love of food and a passion for reducing food waste. However, because I have not had formal training in food preparation, I have been able to throw away the cooking rule books and try incorporating parts of ingredients that many chefs would frown at. Focaccia baked with onion skins – why not? Salsa made with roasted whole kiwis – show me the nachos! And parsnips blended into cheeze – yes please! I hope you also have fun experimenting.

How to use this book

Think of this book as your compleating encyclopaedia. Each chapter is dedicated to a different fruit, vegetable or herb with advice about its nutrients, how best to store and preserve it, when it's in season and how to cook and compleat the whole ingredient, including the parts we usually discard. I've also included ideas for using these in your home and garden. The icons throughout show which parts of the produce can be used – like peels [icon] cores [icon] or seeds [icon] – making it easy for you to look up, for example, apples, and then cores. (See Key on page 4)

Each chapter is full of recipes and advice. I've included "compleat" recipes that make use of the whole ingredient in one dish, as well as useful tips for cooking with each individual part of the food. I recommend using this book as a guide to dip in and out of when you're cooking, shopping, growing or looking for foodie inspiration.

Thank you for supporting this book. I would love to see what you cook! Share your photos with me on Instagram @compleatly_vegan and @ellen_tout and on Twitter @Ellen_Tout with #VeganCompleating. For more, see ellentout.com.

Apples and pears

There are over 7,000 different varieties of apples and thousands of distinct types of pears, but we tend to only see the same handful of colours and flavours in our shops. As well as their sweet flesh, apple and pear peels and even cores can be used to create sauces, dressings and confectionery in your kitchen.

IN SEASON: September – February

MAKE IT LAST! Apples and pears should be stored in the fridge. However, pears are often best purchased when firm or underripe so that they can ripen at room temperature before being stored in the fridge. You could also chop and freeze apples and pears to later add to crumbles.

If you grow or forage a large quantity of apples, then these can be stored somewhere cool on an apple rack for a few months. You can make your own by wrapping each fruit in newspaper and storing them in a cardboard box with a sheet of paper between each layer, making sure the fruits don't touch. Check regularly to remove any bad apples and you'll be enjoying your harvest well into the winter.

NUTRITIONAL BENEFITS: Apples are rich in antioxidants and are a great source of fibre, especially in the skin. They are also a source of vitamins A, C, K and B7. Pears are also a good source of fibre, as well as potassium, phosphorus, vitamin K and calcium.

Apples and pears were named as part of the "dirty dozen" in recent research.[1] This means that unfortunately they are high on the list of produce with multiple pesticide residues, so it's especially worth buying organic or growing your own, and washing the fruit well.

EDIBLE AND USEFUL PARTS: Flesh, peel and core.

1 Pesticide Action Network UK, *Pesticides in Our Food* report, 2017.

Flesh

We tend to eat apples and pears raw and as a quick snack, but try adding chopped raw apple or apple peels to a coleslaw (pages 63–4) or beet slaw (page 37). Slightly old fruits are ideal for stewing or adding to skin-on fruit crumbles, pies or tarts.

Dried apples or pears: Cut the fruit into slices, as thinly as possible, leaving the skin on. Most people core the fruit before doing this, but you can leave the centre intact, only removing seeds or any especially tough parts. Spread evenly on a baking tray and cook at 100°C/200°F/gas mark ½ for 2–3 hours, until fully dried. Eat as a snack or topping for smoothie bowls, granola (pages 238–9) and desserts. Follow this same process with different fruits, like apricots and kiwi, and ideally bake one big batch of dried fruits at once. Store in a jar for up to a month.

Apple sauce: As well as being a condiment, apple sauce is a brilliant replacement for eggs in vegan baking. To make, chop two medium apples into small chunks. There's no real need to remove the peels, but if you are going to use this as an egg replacement you might prefer to - or just use a hand blender to purée the peels into the finished sauce. Add the apples to a saucepan over a medium heat with ¼ teaspoon cinnamon, or more to taste. Once it simmers, reduce the heat and cook for around 20 minutes. Mix in one teaspoon lemon juice and remove from the heat. Use a potato masher or hand blender to purée the sauce, depending on your preference and intended use. Store in a jar in the fridge for a week or freeze.

Chutneys and ferments: Chutneys are a great way to make use of a large amount of apples and pears. I like to forage these, as well as plums, and give the chutneys away as gifts. For my green tomato and apple chutney recipe, turn to pages 225-6.

⌧ Peel

Many dishes, like crumbles or sweet pies, taste great with the apple or pear peels intact. However, others, such as chutneys, do benefit from peeling. The peels are a good source of fibre and well worth saving. These recipes work best fresh, but I also have a tub in our freezer, where we store leftover apple and pear peels and cores. Once you collect enough, these are perfect for making homemade vinegar or syrup. You could also add your chopped peels to homemade granola (pages 238–9) before it goes in the oven.

Apple or pear peel tea: Steep your peels in boiling water, or simmer on the stove, and add ground cinnamon and brown sugar to taste. You could also use a little sweetener in place of sugar, or add some lemon juice. Enjoy warm or cooled in the fridge with ice.

Sweet apple or pear peel crisps: These are best made when the peels are fresh, so the flavour is absorbed. Great as a snack or in granola (pages 238-9). In a bowl, mix 80g/2¾oz peels with one teaspoon sugar and ¼ teaspoon ground cinnamon. Make sure the peels are well coated. Spread evenly on a baking tray and cook at 150°C/300°F/gas mark 2 for 20-30 minutes, checking regularly. The finished peels should be crispy but not burned.

Infuse spirits: Apple and pear peels can be used to infuse spirits. Find my simple recipe on pages 235-6 and experiment with combinations like apple and rhubarb gin or pear vodka.

▣ Core

Apple seeds are poisonous in large quantities. However, you can carefully munch your apple or pear right up to the very centre, avoiding seeds, and leaving just the overly fibrous parts behind. Store whole cores in the freezer with peels until you collect enough to make a vinegar or syrup.

Apple cider or perry vinegar: Cider vinegar, made from apples, or perry vinegar, made from pears, is easy to make using leftover peels and cores. You just need a little patience! Place around ten apple or pear cores in a clean (but not soapy) jar, as well as any peels, and add one tablespoon of sugar. Add enough water to cover the fruit and stir well. It's important that every time you stir you use a clean utensil to avoid any contamination. Place a piece of muslin cloth/cheesecloth over the top of the jar and secure it using a rubber band. Place on a shelf out of direct sunlight and stir every day. After a few weeks it will taste a little like cider/perry. Frothy white bubbles should form on the surface; this is a good sign. But any mould means the batch should be discarded. After around a month, strain out and compost the apple or pear pieces. Cover the jar and leave for another month, after which time it should taste more vinegar-like and is ready to bottle and use. Store this in the fridge for up to a year. It may need to be "burped" every now and then to release any air so keep an eye out for bubbles. If you want to speed up this process, add a "mother" from a shop-bought raw, unfiltered and unpasteurized cider/perry vinegar, or from a batch made previously.

Baked Cinnamon Apples

This traditional pudding lets you savour the apple's natural sweetness and flavour. It takes hardly any time to make and uses kitchen staples. Delicious served warm with plant-based vanilla ice cream.

Prep 5 minutes. **Cooking** 30 mins

- 1 large apple
- 2 tablespoons dark brown sugar
- 3 teaspoons sultanas/golden raisins
- ¼ teaspoon ground cinnamon
- ½ teaspoon finely diced unpeeled root ginger
- ½ teaspoon maple, agave or golden syrup to bind
- Small knob of plant butter
- Plant-based vanilla ice cream, to serve

1   Preheat the oven to 180°C/350°F/gas mark 4.

2   Remove the core from your apple using an apple corer. If possible, do this cautiously so that the base of the apple remains intact. Alternatively, carefully use a knife to remove the core. If there is any apple flesh attached to the removed core, retain and dice this into the filling. Save the core for making apple cider vinegar or compost it.

3   In a bowl, mix the sugar, sultanas, cinnamon, root ginger and sweetener until combined. You can also add any offcut apple flesh or diced apple or pear peel from making other dishes. Stuff this filling into the centre of the apple, using your fingers to compress it down and ensure it is tightly packed.

4   Place the apple in an ovenproof dish with a very shallow layer of water. If you have any other apple or pear peels or flesh to use up, you can chop and add these to the dish around the apple. Top the apple with the butter.

5   Bake in the preheated oven for 25–30 minutes until softened. Serve warm with ice cream. Drizzle over any syrup or fruit that has collected in the dish.

Asparagus

Asparagus is at its best for just a few months of the year and yet so much of each spear is usually wasted. The whole asparagus is edible and, unless very old, is flavoursome. Steam, grill/broil, barbeque, stir-fry, enjoy raw or on a pizza. Here are some of my favourite more unusual recipes to help you rethink the way you cook this plant.

IN SEASON: April – June

MAKE IT LAST! If possible, buy local and fresh so that the whole asparagus will be tasty and more delicate. Ideally eat asparagus on the day you purchase it. To keep a bunch crisp, stand it in a jar of water in the fridge.

NUTRITIONAL BENEFITS: Asparagus is rich in folate, which helps produce and maintain new cells, as well as vitamins A, C and K. Research has also shown asparagus to have anti-inflammatory properties.

Asparagus was named as part of the "dirty dozen" in recent research. This means that unfortunately they are high on the list of produce with multiple pesticide residues, so it's especially worth buying organic or growing your own, if you can, and washing your asparagus well.

EDIBLE AND USEFUL PARTS: Whole spear and stalk ends.

▦ Whole spear

The rule that we should bend a spear of asparagus until it breaks, discarding the snapped off stalk end, is untrue. Asparagus actually breaks at its weakest point and much of the stalk end is edible and flavoursome. I often eat the whole spear, but a good rule of thumb is to nip off and test a little of the stalk end, working your way up the spear until you find a texture you are happy with. Any ends you do remove can be used in soups or sliced very thinly into dishes like risotto and stew.

Asparagus risotto: I love making risotto with mushrooms, asparagus and peas. The stalk ends of the asparagus spears can be finely chopped and added at the same time as the arborio rice so that they soften and impart their flavour to the dish. The spears can then be added a few minutes before your dish has finished cooking.

▣ Stalk ends

I often save asparagus ends and chop them thinly into various different dishes. A common recipe to use them up is in a soup or broth, but I prefer to incorporate them into things like risotto, stew, stir-fry and my falafel recipe, where they add a little bite and a lovely flavour.

Falafels with asparagus ends: Collect the offcut stalk ends from a bunch of asparagus. These are best fresh. Slice each piece into quarters lengthways and then dice thinly. Dice one garlic clove and sauté in a pan with the chopped asparagus ends in one teaspoon of rapeseed/canola oil for a few minutes to soften. Drain a 400g/14oz can of chickpeas/garbanzo beans (save the aquafaba, see pages 83–90). In a bowl, mash the chickpeas to break them down but not purée them. Add the asparagus ends and garlic, plus a handful of chopped fresh parsley, one tablespoon tomato purée/paste, ½ teaspoon ground cumin, ¼ teaspoon sriracha and one tablespoon plain/all-purpose flour. Season with salt and pepper and mix well. In a frying pan, heat one teaspoon of rapeseed/canola oil. Divide the falafel mix into eight to ten pieces and roll into slightly flat balls. Cook these in the oil for a few minutes each side over a medium to high heat so that the sides are browned and the centre hot. A satisfying alternative to traditional falafels.

Compleat Recipe: Veg Royale Brunch with Asparagus, Smoked Carrot Lox and Scrambled Tofu

This brunch is my plant-based take on eggs royale. Perfect for impressing guests or sharing a delicious brunch with your partner. The smoked "salmon" style carrot lox can be prepared in advance and left to marinade overnight, but if you're short of time then dive straight in.

Prep 30 minutes, plus marinating
Cooking 25 mins **Serves** 4

For the smoked "salmon" style carrot lox:
- 1–2 carrots
- 2 tablespoons olive oil
- 4 teaspoons light soy sauce
- 2 teaspoons liquid smoke
- 1 teaspoon of brine from a jar of capers
- 1 teaspoon lemon juice
- 1 sheet of sushi nori, crumbled
- ½ teaspoon sea salt
- A little black pepper

For the scrambled tofu:
- ½ teaspoon rapeseed/canola oil
- 400g/14oz block firm unpressed organic tofu
- ¼ teaspoon ground turmeric
- 1 teaspoon garlic powder
- ½ teaspoon smoked paprika
- ½ teaspoon black salt powder/ kala namak

To serve:
- Bunch of asparagus (around 3 spears per person)
- 4 English muffins, sliced in half
- Plant butter
- A little lemon juice

1 Prepare the smoked "salmon" style carrot lox as per the recipe on pages 66-7. Ideally leave these to marinade overnight, then bake for 10–15 minutes while preparing the tofu.

2 Heat the oil in a frying pan over a medium heat and crumble in the tofu to achieve a scrambled consistency. Add the turmeric, garlic powder and smoked paprika and mix well. Cook for around 7 minutes, mixing occasionally, until the tofu is cooked but not crispy. One minute before removing from the heat, add the black salt powder and mix well, ensuring the salt does not clump.

3 Cook the asparagus whole or slice off the very end and save to make soup or stock, depending on its texture. In a lidded pan, heat 60ml/2fl oz/¼ cup water and add the asparagus. Steam for 3–4 minutes, then remove from the heat. Whilst steaming, toast the muffins.

4 To serve, butter the toasted muffins and cover each half with the scrambled tofu. Top with the carrot lox and asparagus. Squeeze a little lemon juice over each. Any leftover marinade from the carrots can also be drizzled over.

Aubergine/eggplant

With their distinctive flavour, aubergines are brilliant in Asian and Mediterranean cuisine. As well as the deep purple variety, they grow in an assortment of different colours and sizes. You can compleat the whole aubergine fruit, but avoid any leaves or stalk.

IN SEASON: May – October

MAKE IT LAST! Aubergines are best stored in the fridge and can also be cooked and frozen or pickled.

NUTRITIONAL BENEFITS:
Aubergines are a great source of vitamins B1 and B6, as well as fibre, potassium and the minerals copper, magnesium and manganese. They are also rich in antioxidants – nasunin, in particular, is found in aubergine skin.

EDIBLE AND USEFUL PARTS:
Flesh, skin and seeds.

⌷⟁ Flesh and skin

Aubergine has a unique flavour – creamy and slightly sweet. To get the most from your aubergine's flesh, lift up the small leaves and cut right to the very end. I like to add this small piece of stalk and leaves to a tub for making mixed veggie offcuts broth (page 232–4). However, these should only be used in small amounts as they are a member of the nightshade family. If you grow your own aubergines and have an abundance to preserve, try pickling them in chunks with some garlic and dried oregano (page 235), or slice and roast them and freeze ready to add to dishes.

☑ My favourite ways to compleat:

Baked aubergine parmigiana: Aubergines are delicious in a ratatouille with courgette/zucchini, garlic, onions and tomatoes (recipe on page 117). I also love making an Italian parmigiana. Thinly slice an aubergine lengthways and griddle each slice for a few minutes with a little olive oil before layering it in an ovenproof dish with homemade oven roasted tomato sauce (recipe on page 223) between each layer. Top with plant-based cheeze and bake in the oven at 180°C/350°F/gas mark 4 for 20 minutes. Great served with garlic bread to soak up the sauce.

Roasted aubergine topped dahl: Aubergine melts in the mouth when chopped, coated in curry powder and roasted with a little rapeseed/canola oil at 190°C/375°F/gas mark 5 for 25 minutes. It makes a flavoursome topping for a lentil dahl.

Aubergine baba ganoush: This Middle Eastern dip is creamy and rich and is great with a mezze. However, most recipes discard the aubergine skin. On pages 129-30 of the garlic chapter, my baba ganoush recipe uses two whole aubergines, roasted with garlic cloves. The ingredients are blended into a delicious dip, skin and all.

Avocado

It's fair to say that plant eaters love avocados! Ripe but firm, they are ideal for a salad, and once softened, who doesn't love them on toast, crackers or as guacamole? The jury is still out about whether the stone and skins are safe to eat, but why not upcycle them as a natural fabric dye or to grow your own avocado houseplant?

IN SEASON: Available year-round, but it's also worth considering the carbon footprint of tropical fruits like this.

MAKE IT LAST! Avocados are best stored at room temperature until ripe. Once ripe, store your avocados in the fridge. To speed up the ripening process, place your avocados in a brown paper bag with a banana. The most common variety, the Hass avocado, is ripe when the skin changes to a very dark green colour. You can also check by gently squeezing the avocado – it should be soft but not overly squidgy. If you only eat half of an avocado (not a problem I've ever had!), then squeeze a little lemon or lime juice over the other half, wrap it in aluminium foil and store it in the fridge for a day or two to help keep it fresh.

NUTRITIONAL BENEFITS: Avocados are full of goodness and are a great source of vitamins B6, E and K, as well as folate, fibre and minerals like iron, copper and potassium. Avocados also contain monounsaturated fats, which can help care for your heart's health.

EDIBLE AND USEFUL PARTS:
Flesh, skin and stone.

⬚ Flesh

Creamy and satisfying, enjoy avocado smashed on toast with salt, pepper, chilli flakes and roasted pumpkin seeds. I love adding wedges of avocado to a salad or Buddha bowl, or as a topping for tacos, chilli or my vegan huevos rancheros Mexican brunch (recipe on pages 95–7). When preparing your avocado, use a spoon to scoop out as much flesh as possible, right up to the skin.

Avocado mousse: Avocado makes a smooth, rich dessert when mixed with a few simple ingredients. Melt one bar (100g/3½oz) of dark vegan chocolate and set aside to cool a little. Remove the skin and stones from two avocados and mash the flesh in a bowl or food processor until smooth and creamy. Add the melted chocolate and mix well until fully combined. Taste a little and add some sweetener, such as maple or agave syrup if you wish, or a little cocoa powder for a richer taste. Divide the mixture between four ramekins and place in the fridge to chill for at least 30 minutes. Serve with a few shavings of dark chocolate grated over the top.

Griddled avocado: We tend to think of avocado as best served chilled, but the flavour is slightly smoky and really tasty when griddled or cooked over a barbeque. Slice your avocado in half and remove the stone but leave the skin on. Brush the avocado flesh with a little olive oil. Heat a griddle pan until very hot or cook over a barbeque. Place the avocado halves, flesh down, on the pan/barbeque. Cook for a few minutes until warm and lightly charred. To serve, remove the shell and serve on a bed of chopped lettuce, tomatoes and cucumber with a drizzle of olive oil. You also have the option to griddle some tomato, onion and pepper slices at the same time as cooking the avocado.

Guacamole: This classic Mexican dip can easily be adjusted to suit your taste and what you have available in your kitchen on that day. As a guide, mash the flesh of two ripe avocados in a bowl or pestle and mortar with half a diced red onion, one diced garlic clove, a handful of chopped fresh coriander/cilantro, half a diced red chilli, a generous squeeze of lime and some salt and pepper. Try serving it with homemade tortilla chips (pags 43-3) and my pineapple core or kiwi salsa (recipes on page 149-50).

Stone and skin

There have been claims that both the avocado stone and skin are edible – blended into smoothies, grated as seasoning or roasted. However, there has yet to be any research to show that these are safe to eat so I recommend avoiding them. The taste is quite bitter and the proclaimed health benefits have not been proven. However, woodworkers have started using the stones to carve into amazing jewellery, buttons and artwork. They can also be used to make a natural dye or to plant.

Household projects and ideas

Natural fabric dye: Avocado stones and skins can be used to create a natural fabric dye with beautiful shades of pink. Collect the cleaned stones and skins in the freezer or dried out on a plate on a windowsill until you have five to ten saved. The riper the avocado, the better the dye should be - you'll notice how the avocado skin changes colour. Wash any avocado flesh off the stones and skin before using as this could turn the dye brown.

Place these in a large pan of water and bring to the boil. Use a low heat so that the colour is slowly released, rather than cooked. Simmer gently for a few hours but check regularly to see if you are happy with the shade of the water. It should turn a lovely deep pink or red. Once ready, turn off the

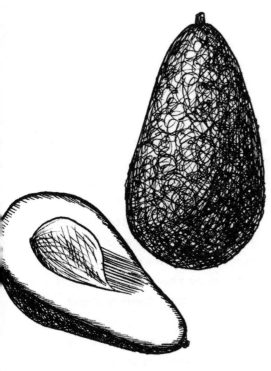

heat to strain out the avocado and compost it.

You can use this liquid to fully colour fabrics, but it's fun to experiment with a natural tie dye effect. Natural fabrics work best. Scrunch your fabric or clothing into the desired tie dye pattern and fix with elastic bands. Carefully submerge your piece in the water, ensuring it is fully covered. Leave it to absorb the dye for eight hours, or longer if you wish. You can check on the results and colour as you go. When you're happy, unwrap the fabric and rinse under cold water. Leave to hang dry and you're done!

Unlike onion skins (pages 169–71), avocado dye doesn't contain a natural fixative so the colour will fade a little over time. A mordant can be used to help seal in the colour, but for expert natural dyeing advice, I recommend the work of a vegan natural dyer like Rebecca Desnos.

🌱 How to Grow an Avocado Plant from the Stone

Successfully growing an avocado plant from the stone seems to have become the stuff of legends. Follow these steps and, fingers crossed, you should be rewarded with a beautiful houseplant. We have managed to grow a few of these mini trees at home, one of which is over two years old and quickly outgrowing our windowsill! To boost your success rate, I recommend trying a few of these at once.

You'll need

To start:
- At least 1 avocado stone
- Glass jars
- Cocktail sticks

Once developed:
- Plant pots
- Compost or soil

1   Remove the stone from your avocado (eat the flesh as normal). Rinse and wipe the stone clean, removing as much of the avocado flesh as possible.

2   Fill a small jar three-quarters of the way full of water. Make sure you know which is the top of your stone – the base should be flatter, and the slightly pointed top should face upward. The aim is for your avocado stone to sit over the jar of water, with the base submerged up to about one third of the stone.

3   Using three to four cocktail sticks, insert them into the stone at roughly a 45-degree angle, rather than horizontal, to make a kind of tripod support. If the stone has any natural ridge lines, where it might naturally split and sprout, don't insert the sticks at those points.

4   Place your jar, with the stone resting in the water, on a windowsill. This is a slow process, but the stone should start to split almost in half after a few weeks. From the crater, a root will shoot down and the plant will begin to sprout up. Check and refresh the water once a week and don't allow any mould to form.

5   After one to three months, the roots should be well established. Transfer to a larger jar with water, set up in the same way. I have allowed the roots to be around 15cm/6in long before transferring the plant to a pot, but you could do so a little sooner if the plant looks healthy and fairly robust.

6   Next, it's time to move your plant to a pot. The roots may now be fairly long and spiralling around the jar. To plant, fill a medium-sized pot with a little compost. Test to see if the roots will fit with enough space to develop further. The stone should not be fully buried and should sit with the top half exposed above the soil, similar to in the jar. Remove the cocktail sticks. Be very careful when transferring the plant to the pot – the roots are delicate. Once the roots are securely in the pot, fill with compost or soil, making sure to compact it well around the stone. Give your plant a little water.

7   Avocado plants thrive in warm, humid conditions. Our plants have flourished on our bathroom windowsill, because this mimics their natural environment. Water your avocado plant a little every week, or once the top levels of soil are dry. Repot as and when needed. Whilst it is unlikely that your avocado plants will develop fruit, they make a beautiful houseplant and are a great talking point with guests.

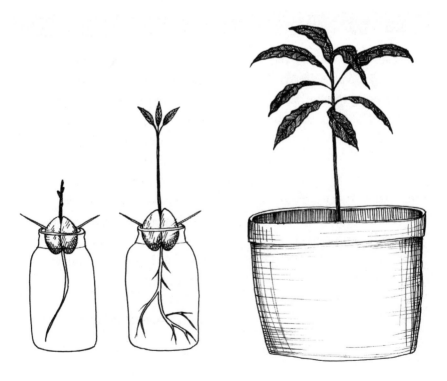

Banana

Bananas are the UK's most popular fruit and yet around one million are thrown out every day – often because they are deemed too green or too brown![1] You can store green bananas in a brown bag to speed up ripening. If your bananas are brown, they are perfect for making banana bread, ice cream, smoothies or adding to a coconutty curry.

---

1 Wrap, Food surplus and waste in the UK – key facts report, updated January 2020.

IN SEASON: Available all year, but it's also worth considering the carbon footprint of tropical fruits like this.

MAKE IT LAST! Bananas are best stored at room temperature. Store away from other fruits as the plant hormones in bananas can cause other produce to ripen – useful if you have an underripe avocado!

NUTRITIONAL BENEFITS: Bananas are an excellent source of potassium, which contributes to regulating heart function and blood pressure. They also contain fibre and vitamins B6 and C. The peels are especially high in potassium, as well as containing protein, fibre and the mood-boosting hormone serotonin.

EDIBLE AND USEFUL PARTS: Flesh and peel.

Tip: My local farm shop gives away really brown bananas for free – so keep an eye out for any to rescue.

▣ Flesh

Banana is a brilliant energy source raw or added to dishes. The white stringy bits that you usually peel off and discard are called phloem bundles and are actually edible and flavoursome. Eat these fresh with the fruit, blend into smoothies or mash into banana bread with the flesh.

Banana nice cream: This is so simple to make and perfect for overripe bananas. Chop them into chunks and freeze. When ready, blend them for a few seconds in a food processor. Serve as is or add flavourings like peanut butter, vanilla extract, cocoa powder and maple syrup. Best eaten immediately. This can be frozen but the moisture in the banana can cause it to crystalize and form a hard block. To solve this, blend in a food processor again or whip with a fork before serving.

Banana pancakes: Browner bananas are perfect for adding to pancakes. They can be mashed into your batter, but I prefer to slice them and add to the pan with your batter so that they caramelize a little. See pages 211–12 for my strawberry pancakes recipe and cook the banana slices using the same method as for the strawberries.

Smoothies: Bananas are a great addition to smoothies with oats, peanut butter, dates and plant milk. A good way to use up browner bananas, you can also chop and freeze these to blend from frozen into smoothies and shakes. Don't forget to add the white stringy parts known as the phloem bundles – these are nutritious and tasty once blended.

⌕ Peel

In some parts of the world, banana skin is commonly eaten – especially amongst vegan communities because it absorbs flavour well and can be manipulated to create different textures. Slice off the very ends and wash well before cooking. Browner peels work best for these recipes as green peels are too bitter. Peels can be collected and saved in an airtight container in the fridge for a few days until you are ready to use them.

Banana peel "bacon": Choose yellow to brown peels. To prepare the peels, wash them, remove the hard ends and separate into long strips 2.5–5cm/1–2in wide. Use a spoon to scrape off the phloem bundles (save these for a smoothie if you wish). You should now have thin strips ready to marinade. In a bowl mix one tablespoon dark soy sauce, two teaspoons maple syrup, one teaspoon water, ½ teaspoon garlic powder and ½ teaspoon smoked paprika to create the smoky, salty and sweet taste. Coat the banana skins and leave to marinade for at least 20 minutes. I like to make this the night before, ready for breakfast. When ready, heat one tablespoon rapeseed/canola oil in a frying pan over a medium to high heat. Fry each piece of peel for a few minutes on each side to reach the desired texture - it can be left to go crispy or softer, to taste.

Barbeque pulled banana peel: A great alternative to jackfruit, these peels are sweet and smoky. Enjoy in a burger bun or pitta bread with homemade coleslaw (pages 63–4). Also try adding them to tacos or as a topping for pizza. You'll need one to two banana peels per person, depending on their size. Wash the peels, remove the hard ends and use the back of a spoon to scrape off the phloem bundles (save these for a smoothie if you wish). Run a fork along the length of each piece of banana skin to "pull" it into fine strips. You can use a knife to encourage this. Now, make the sauce. This recipe makes enough for two medium banana peels. In a bowl, mix two tablespoons tomato purée/paste, two teaspoons maple syrup, one teaspoon water, one teaspoon smoked paprika, ½ teaspoon rapeseed/canola oil, ¼ teaspoon sriracha, ¼ teaspoon ground cinnamon, ¼ teaspoon onion powder, ¼ teaspoon garlic powder and a tiny pinch of salt. Add the pulled skins and coat well. This can be left to marinade or cooked immediately. In a frying pan, heat a splash of water over a medium heat. Add the coated peels and stir well. Cook for around five minutes. Browner skins tend to cook faster so stir and check frequently. Add more water or allow more time if needed. When ready, the peels should be tender to bite but not mushy. Serve hot.

• **A note about banana peel:** If you take prescription monoamine oxidase inhibitors then you should not eat banana peel, as well as things like broad/fava beans, some soy-based products like soy sauce and miso, and fermented foods like sauerkraut and kimchi. If you're unsure, please seek professional medical advice.

Banana Peel Bean Burgers

This recipe came about almost by accident whilst I was experimenting with whether I could create veggie balls from banana peels. The subtle sweetness of the peels balances brilliantly with the spicy beans to create tasty patties that are more exciting than your typical bean burger.

Choose yellow to brown banana peels and wash before use.

Prep 15 minutes. **Cooking** 10 minutes
Makes 4 large burgers

- 4 banana skins (yellow to brown)
- 400g/14oz can red kidney beans in chilli sauce
- 1 white onion, diced
- 1 teaspoon dried mixed herbs
- ½ teaspoon ground cumin
- ½ teaspoon smoked paprika
- ½ teaspoon garlic powder
- 100g/3½oz/2/3 cup plain/ all-purpose flour
- Salt and black pepper
- 2-3 teaspoons rapeseed/canola oil
- Burger buns, pitta breads and/or salad, to serve

1   Prepare the banana skins by washing them, removing the hard ends and using a spoon to scrape off the phloem bundles (save these for a smoothie if you wish). Chop the peels into small pieces, roughly 1cm/½in squares.

2   Empty the kidney beans and sauce into a bowl and use a fork or masher to break down the beans a little, but not to a purée. Add the onion, herbs and spices, chopped banana peels and flour. Season and mix well until combined.

3   In a frying pan, heat the oil. Divide the burger mix into four large patties or eight smaller ones. Add to the pan and cook over a medium heat for a few minutes each side – around seven to ten minutes in total. The burgers should be crispy on the outside and hot inside. Serve with a bun, pitta bread and/or salad, to taste.

☑ My favourite ways to compleat:

Banana bread using peels and flesh: Brown banana peels can be washed, chopped, simmered and blended to produce a sweet purée. This is perfect for adding to a banana bread or other cakes, alongside or as an alternative to mashed banana flesh. Turn to pages 118–19 for my banana peel and courgette loaf cake recipe.

Barbequed bananas with chocolate: These were one of my favourite treats as a child and are perfect for camping trips or to make the most of the heat from a barbeque after cooking your savoury dishes. To prepare, slice each banana, in its skin, down the length. Pop a handful of chunks of vegan chocolate into the flesh. Wrap each banana in aluminium foil and bake over the barbeque for around ten minutes until the chocolate is melted and the fruit soft and warm. Simple but so satisfying. Use a spoon to scoop out all the chocolatey banana and eat directly from the fruit. The phloem bundles go all gooey so can be eaten and the skin helps seal in the juices – you can also eat this or choose to compost.

Green-fingered ideas

Banana peels can be chopped up and buried in your garden and will release nutrients into the soil as they decompose. It is also believed that chopping the peels and burying them around the base of a plant helps to deter aphids, if topped up regularly.

Wellbeing uses

Banana peels have traditionally been used to soothe insect stings by rubbing the flesh over the affected area. The same technique has also been used as a home remedy to help remove warts. My mum swore by this and it really did work! Cut the peel into a square big enough to cover the wart, secure with tape or a plaster and leave overnight. Repeat every night for a few weeks and you should see results.

Plaintain

Plantain skin is also edible. It doesn't have much flavour but absorbs marinades well. Try it shredded through a spicy stir fry or enjoy it pulled as you would banana skin.

Beer & wine

The idea of surplus beer or wine may seem unlikely, but if you open a bottle you dislike, don't quite finish or have left over after a gathering, don't let it go to waste. If you're not going to cook with the alcohol any time soon then pour it into ice cube trays and freeze it ready to use later.

Beer

Ales work best but all beers can be added to dishes like stews, stroganoff, marinades and beer batter or mixed into a punchy barbeque sauce. Interestingly, the origins and ingredients in beer and bread are very similar – so you can actually use beer as a substitute for yeast and water when baking bread.

How to save leftover beer: Store beer bottles upright, and in the fridge if opened, so that the beer comes into as little contact as possible with any air in the bottle - this will help slow down oxidization and keep your beer fresh. It can also be decanted and frozen in ice cube trays for cooking.

Easy vegan beer batter: In a bowl, mix 180g/6¼oz/1 1/3 cups plain/all-purpose flour with one teaspoon cornflour/cornstarch, one teaspoon onion powder, ½ teaspoon garlic powder and ½ teaspoon ground cumin. Pour in 300ml/10½fl oz/1¼ cups ale and mix well using a hand whisk. Use to batter tofu, tofish, vegan sausages or mushrooms.

🍺 Wine

Once opened, wine starts to oxidise and, if left too long, it can start to taste bitter. Leftover wine can be added to dishes like stews, pasta sauce and risotto. You could also add a little wine to a vegan jelly or trifle – adults only! Or wake up slightly old white wine with some lemonade to make a refreshing spritzer. Interestingly, adding a little leftover wine to a compost heap every now and then can help promote decomposition.

Homemade wine vinegar: This is delicious added to dressings and, if left long enough, can also be used for pickling. To make it, you'll need at least half a bottle of red or white wine. Pour this into a large jar, ensuring there is some space for air, and seal the top with a piece of muslin cloth/cheesecloth, secured with a rubber band. Place on a shelf, somewhere not too light, and that's it. Wait a few months, or up to six, whilst the magic happens, and it ferments. Check on it regularly. If you see a rather gross looking gelatinous disk appear at the top, then that's good news – it's the "mother". This should sink when your vinegar is ready. You can speed the process up by adding a "mother" from a shop-bought raw, unfiltered and unpasteurized wine or cider vinegar. If so, use a ratio of two parts wine to one part shop-bought vinegar, and wait a few months. When ready, it will taste vinegary and tangy. Decant into a bottle, where it will continue to mature as you use it. A great tip is to leave a little of this in the fermenting jar to act as your own new "mother", which can be used to speed up making your next batch of vinegar. You can even add any wine dregs to that jar to start the process again and keep it going.

Beetroot

As a child, I loved eating the beetroots my parents grew by the bucketload – turning my face pink in the process. I've since continued the tradition by growing my own, but discarding the beautiful foliage on top of the root felt like half the plant was wasted. When we buy beets pickled or packaged from a shop, this has often already been trimmed off – but there's so much more to this vegetable.

IN SEASON: July – January

MAKE IT LAST! Fresh beetroot is best stored whole in the fridge. The leaves can also be stored in the fridge or chopped and frozen, ready to later add to stews and curries as you would spinach.

NUTRITIONAL BENEFITS: Beetroots are incredibly nutritious, especially the leaves and stalks. Beet greens are rich in iron and calcium, as well as vitamins A and C.

The whole beetroot is a source of folate and fibre. They have been found to be antioxidant, and studies have shown that they may have blood pressure lowering properties.

Beetroots were named as part of the "clean 15" in recent research. This means that they were found to contain little, if any, pesticide residues!

EDIBLE AND USEFUL PARTS: Flesh, skin, stalks and leaves/tops.

▣ Flesh

Sweet and earthy when cooked, but tarter when raw, beetroot is a versatile delight. Roast or boil whole and enjoy. If boiling, the water will turn a bright pink-purple colour. This broth is rich in nutrients, taste and colour. Save it to use as stock for soup or pink risotto; or as a natural food colouring for things like icing. This water can also be used to pickle turnips – in Middle Eastern cuisine it is beetroots that traditionally give the turnips their bright colour (recipe on pages 228–9).

Whole boiled or roasted beetroots: Whether roasting or boiling your beetroots, leave the skin on. Recipes often say to remove this but there's usually no need. It sometimes naturally peels off when boiling – if so, collect and blitz it into a smoothie. I also like to leave 2.5cm/1in of stalk attached. Depending on their size, allow 40 minutes to one hour to boil or roast your beetroots, until knife soft. If roasting, coat in a little oil and optional seasoning like a whole garlic clove or sprig of rosemary and cook at 190°C/375°F/gas mark 5.

Pickled beets: Roast or boil your beetroots, as above, and place in a jar with the ingredients for my easy pickle recipe, found on page 235. You could include a mix of cooked beetroot and raw beet stalks. I leave the skin on and a short piece of stalk attached when pickling. If you boil your beets first, then use the purple water to add extra flavour and colour to your pickle. Beetroots can also be thinly sliced to ferment and make a sauerkraut with other vegetables, like cabbage or turnips (page 62).

Beet brownies: Grate boiled beetroots into your favourite plant-based brownie recipe to create a naturally sweet and moist bake. You may need to cook for slightly longer to compensate for the added liquid, but the result is an amazingly squidgy and moreish brownie.

🖉Leaves

Whilst the leaves are edible, the taste varies
with the plant's age and size. Smaller young
leaves are sweeter and tasty raw in salads. Older
large leaves can be a little bitter raw so shred these
and use sparingly raw or sauté them. Much like
spinach leaves, beet greens shrink when cooked
and can be added to curries, soups and stews in
place of other greens.

Beet leaf crisps: Wash and dry the leaves of a bunch of
beetroots. Leave the stalks of small leaves attached and
remove any larger stalks. Preheat the oven to 180°C/350°F/
gas mark 4. Toss the leaves in enough oil to lightly coat them
and season with salt and pepper. Spread evenly on a baking
tray and cook for roughly five minutes, checking regularly
to ensure the leaves don't burn. Follow these same steps
to make crisps from any leftover beetroot peelings.

Sautéed beet leaves and stalks: Thinly slice a medium-sized bunch of beet
leaves and stalks. In a pan, heat ½ teaspoon olive oil and add two diced
garlic cloves. After one minute, add the leaves and stalks. Stir and season
with salt and pepper. After another three minutes, squeeze over the juice
of ¼ lemon (one teaspoon). Stir and remove from the heat after one
minute. Delicious as a side or stirred through grains.

Beet greens pesto: Use the baby leaves in place of traditional basil to
create a distinctive pesto. See page 158-9 for my salad bag pesto recipe
and use whatever greens you have available, such as beet leaves, carrot
tops or spinach.

⬇ Stalks

Eaten raw, beet stalks can taste bitter. Chop sparingly through a salad or dish; or cook to bring out their sweeter flavour.

Pickled stalks: Chop your stalks into 2.5cm/1in pieces and place in a jar with the ingredients for my easy pickle recipe, found on page 235.

Baked beet stalks: Chop the stalks from a bunch of beetroot into 2.5cm/1in pieces and place in an ovenproof dish. Coat with one teaspoon of olive oil, ½ teaspoon garlic powder and season with salt and pepper. Bake at 180°C/350°F/gas mark 4 for 15 minutes until soft. These are a surprisingly moreish side dish or snack.

☑ My favourite ways to compleat:

Compleat beet slaw: For this raw slaw, grate one large (or two medium) raw beetroots into a bowl with one carrot – both should be washed but not peeled. Finely chop one broccoli stalk (optional, or try an apple) and the whole length of one spring onion/scallion and add to the bowl. Mix and squeeze in the juice of half a lemon. The slaw is ready. If your beetroot had leaves and stalks, then you could also shred these thinly through the slaw.

Compleat Recipe: Roasted Beets with Grains and Greens

Make full use of your beetroots with this wholesome dish. Chopped fresh herbs really bring it to life. I've used quinoa but choose your favourite grains, such as buckwheat or couscous. Great served in a big bowl as an unusual dish to share at a buffet or meal, or as your lunch or dinner.

Prep 20 minutes **Cooking** 40 minutes
Serves 4

- Beetroots (1–2 bunches of 5–8 beetroots, depending on size), raw and with leaves
- 1 tablespoon olive oil
- 250g/9oz dried quinoa
- ½ teaspoon vegetable stock powder/bouillon
- 1 teaspoon lemon juice
- Large handful of fresh parsley (or carrot tops as an alternative), roughly chopped
- Large handful of fresh mint, roughly chopped
- Salt and black pepper

To cook the leaves (optional)
- ½ teaspoon olive oil
- 2 garlic cloves, finely diced
- 1 teaspoon lemon juice

1   Wash the beets and remove the leaves, retaining 2.5cm/1in of stalk on each beetroot. Set the leaves aside and chop the beets (skin on) into 3cm/1¼in dice. Place in an ovenproof dish and coat with the olive oil. Season and roast at 190°C/375°F/gas mark 5 for 30–40 minutes until knife soft.

2   Meanwhile, cook the quinoa (or your choice of grain) in a saucepan with 800ml/28fl oz/3½ cups water and the stock powder/bouillon. Bring to the boil and simmer with the lid on for 10 minutes. Drain and set aside.

3   Next, prepare your beet greens. In a pan, heat the olive oil and garlic for 1 minute. Then add the thinly chopped leaves and stalks. Stir and season. After 3 minutes, add the lemon juice. Stir and remove from the heat after 1 minute.

4   Once your beetroots are roasted, combine the quinoa, greens and beetroots (including any remaining oil from the beetroots) in a large bowl. Stir through the mint and parsley (including the parsley stalks), season with salt and pepper to taste and squeeze over the lemon juice. Mix well and serve.

🐾 Green pet foods

In moderation, steamed beet greens are good for your dog. My dog, Bella, loves steamed veggies like these, carrot ends and chopped broccoli stalks. Wild birds, such as sparrows, love raw beet leaves too.

Berries

The first signs of wild blackberries in the hedgerows always fill me with joy. I love them fresh but also freeze lots to have a winter supply of ingredients for crumble. Berries are so tasty picked straight from a homegrown or wild bush, and we have so many different varieties of berries available to buy – from blueberries to raspberries, gooseberries and mulberries.

IN SEASON: Most berries are in season over summer, including blackberries, raspberries, gooseberries and currants. Both cranberries, which are in season from October to November, and blueberries, are not technically berries. Both tend to be grown in America and warmer European countries.

MAKE IT LAST! Berries are best stored in the fridge and can also be frozen, ready to add to crumbles or pies.

To save space, you could purée an abundance of berries and freeze this in batches in an ice cube tray to add to smoothies, juices or desserts. Berries can also be preserved by dehydrating them.

NUTRITIONAL BENEFITS: Berries are an excellent source of vitamin C and antioxidants, great for boosting immunity and overall health.

EDIBLE AND USEFUL PARTS: Berries and leaves.

⊡ Berries

My favourite way to eat berries is raw, but if they are a bit mushy or past their best then don't throw them out. Try them blended into smoothies, simmered to make jam, cooked into a compôte or baked in a crumble.

Fluffy vegan berry pancakes: In the strawberry chapter (pages 211–12) I've included a recipe for vegan pancakes with strawberries cooked in the batter. Try this recipe using berries such as blueberries, blackberries or raspberries. This is a great way to make use of berries which might be a little past their best.

Berry ice lollies: In a blender, mix one-part plant yogurt with one-part berries of your choice – a mixture or just one variety. You could also include some browned banana. Once smooth, pour into ice lolly moulds and freeze overnight. Once completely frozen, serve and enjoy.

Mint and berry ice cubes: In an ice cube tray, place a few leaves of mint, plus any berries which might need using up into each hole. Fill with water and freeze. Once frozen, add to drinks and cocktails.

French Cinnamon Toast with Berry Compôte

After having French toast at a vegan B&B, I had to make my own. My recipe is sweet and cinnamony, served warm and topped with berries – perfect for a sweet brunch. In French, this is called "*pain perdu*", meaning "lost bread". This is because it was originally made from stale bread and is a great way to use up any bread that is just past its best.

Prep 10 minutes **Cooking** 20 minutes
Serves 2–4

- 80g/¾oz/scant 2/3 cup plain/
  all-purpose flour
- 2 tablespoons light brown sugar
- 1 teaspoon ground cinnamon
- 150ml/5fl oz/scant 2/3 cup
  plant milk
- 1 teaspoon vanilla extract
- 4 teaspoons plant butter, plus extra
  if needed
- 4 slices white bread (fresh or stale)

For the compôte
- 300g/10½oz berries of your choice
- Sugar, to taste
- Squeeze of fresh lemon juice
  (optional)

1   First, make the berry compôte. Place the berries in a saucepan with two tablespoons water. Warm over a medium to low heat so that it simmers gently. Stir frequently and cook for a few minutes so that the berries reduce down and create a sauce. Carefully taste the berries and stir in a little sugar, starting with one teaspoon and adding a little as you go. Also add an optional squeeze of lemon juice. Sweeter berries, like raspberries or blueberries, may not need any sugar, whilst those such as blackberries may need more. Once you're happy, remove from the heat and set aside.

2   In a bowl, use a hand whisk to combine the flour, sugar and cinnamon. Then add the milk and vanilla extract. Use the whisk to mix well and ensure there are no lumps. Make sure your bowl is wide enough to be able to submerge a slice of bread in the batter.

3   In a frying pan, melt half of the plant butter over a medium heat until sizzling. Reduce the heat slightly. Using tongs, dunk one slice of the bread in the batter to fully coat it. Carefully place it in the frying pan and cook for a couple of minutes on each side. Be careful as the bread can go from golden brown to burned very quickly! Cook each of the slices of bread using the same method and replenish the plant butter when needed.

4   Warm the compôte just before serving and drizzle it over the French toast.

🌿 Leaves

If you grow your own berries or like to forage them, you might be surprised to know that the leaves from blackberries, mulberries, raspberries and currants are also edible. Please make sure you are certain you have identified the correct plant! These leaves can be eaten raw when they are very small and young, but are most commonly added to teas, which have traditionally been used for their health benefits.

Berry leaf tea: Teas made using berry leaves are sold in health food shops. You can make your own from blackberry, mulberry, raspberry or currant leaves. Steep a handful of the leaves in boiling water for up to five minutes before straining and drinking. Add a few mint leaves or sweetener to taste.

Stuffed mulberry leaves: Large and free from spikes, mulberry leaves can be stuffed and eaten, just like the leaves from grapevines. On pages 73-4 I've included my recipe for stuffed cauliflower leaves. Follow this as a guide and incorporate your favourite grains and seasonal vegetables into the filling. You could even include some of the mulberries.

☑ My favourite ways to compleat:

Berry-infused spirits: Berries can be used to infuse spirits and you can also include any edible leaves, such as those from blackberries, mulberries and raspberries. Find my simple recipe on pages 235-6. Homemade wild blackberry gin is one of my favourites. I use just the berries, but you could also add a little sugar to taste. Homemade sloe gin is also delicious and is lovely to make over the autumn months.

Bread

Slightly old bread or unwanted ends of a loaf can be turned into breadcrumbs or croutons. White bread makes great panko breadcrumbs, which are useful as a coating for crispy fried tofu or vegetables. Wholemeal bread is better for using as breadcrumbs in stuffing or to crumble over dishes. Also try turning slices of stale white bread into sweet French cinnamon toast (recipe on pages 40–1).

Homemade breadcrumbs: Crumble the bread into small pieces or blitz in a food processor, depending what size you would like your crumbs to be and how you plan to use them. Cook on a baking tray at 180°C/350°F/gas mark 4 for 10–15 minutes until dried and crispy. Store in an airtight container and use within a few months.

Leftover bread croutons: Cut the bread into small cubes, toss in enough olive oil to lightly coat, season with salt, pepper and mixed herbs. Cook on a baking tray at 180°C/350°F/gas mark 4 for around ten minutes, checking they don't burn. Store in an airtight container and use within a few months as a topping for soups and salads.

Waste-free tortilla chips: Make tortilla chips from old tortilla wraps by cutting each wrap into 16 triangles. In a bowl, coat the wraps with ½ tablespoon oil per wrap. I prefer to use olive oil. If you're feeling brave, try a little chilli oil!

Spread evenly on a baking tray and bake at 180°C/350°F/gas mark 4 for around ten minutes, checking they don't burn. Remove from the oven and season generously with salt whilst still hot. Enjoy on their own or serve with homemade salsa (recipe on pages 149–50) or guacamole (recipe on page 22).

Homemade Chestnut, Herb and Stale Bread Stuffing

I love to spend a Sunday afternoon cooking a roasted vegetable dinner, served with homemade Yorkshire puddings, stuffing and mint sauce. This stuffing is made with homemade breadcrumbs, which are a great way to use up old or stale bread, and these can be made in advance and saved in a jar for a few months if you wish. I like to forage sweet chestnuts in autumn, which I peel and store in my freezer, ready to add to dishes like this. However, you can use shop bought chestnuts or replace these with your choice of nuts, such as hazelnuts or walnuts.

Prep 30 minutes **Cooking** 1 hour
Fills one medium 20cm/8in square ovenproof dish

- 2 slices brown or wholemeal bread (or the equivalent pre-prepared as breadcrumbs)
- 100g/3½oz/2/3 cup dried brown lentils
- 1 small white onion, diced
- 2 garlic cloves, finely chopped
- 2 tablespoons plant butter

- Handful of peeled sweet chestnuts or your choice of nuts, such as hazelnuts or walnuts (the equivalent of 5 tablespoons worth when chopped)
- Handful of fresh sage, chopped, or 1 teaspoon dried sage
- Handful of fresh rosemary, chopped, or 1 teaspoon dried
- Up to 400ml/14fl oz/1¾ cups vegetable stock
- Salt and black pepper

1   Make the breadcrumbs by crumbling the bread into small cubes. Spread these evenly on a baking tray and cook in the oven at 180°C/350°F/gas mark 4 for 10–15 minutes until dried and crunchy. Be careful not to overcook or allow these to burn.

2 Meanwhile, simmer the lentils in a pan of boiled water with the lid on over a medium heat for around 15 minutes until softened and cooked. Strain the lentils but save the cooking water to use as a broth for the stuffing.

3 At the same time, sauté the onion and garlic in a pan with one teaspoon of the plant butter for 3 minutes. Add the chestnuts, or nuts, to the pan. Mix and cook for a few minutes, then remove from the heat.

4 Combine the cooked breadcrumbs, lentils, onion, garlic, nuts and herbs in a bowl. Season with a little salt and pepper and stir through one tablespoon melted butter. Mix well and decant into the ovenproof dish.

5 You now need to pour over enough liquid to just cover everything. I use 400ml/14fl oz/1¾ cups of the saved lentil water, but this may vary depending on the size and depth of your tray. If you don't have enough lentil water, supplement this with some stock. Top the stuffing with a few small knobs of the remaining butter.

6 Bake in the oven at 190°C/375°F/gas mark 5 for 20 minutes loosely covered with a sheet of aluminium foil. Then check and uncover the stuffing and bake for a further 10–20 minutes. The stuffing is cooked when the top is brown and crispy and the moisture has reduced but it should not be too dry.

Broad/fava beans and pea pods

Broad beans were among the first cultivated plants, but they don't get the same love today, especially when preparing them can feel like too much trouble. Similarly, we eat bags of frozen peas but rarely buy them when they are beautifully flavoursome and fresh in their pods. However, broad beans and garden peas are edible in their complete form, saving you time and waste. You could also adapt the recipes for mangetout/snow peas, sugar snap peas, French beans or runner beans.

IN SEASON: Broad beans are best over summer, from June to September, and should be eaten fresh and young. Peas have a longer season, from May to November, and should also be as fresh as possible. Both are worth buying from a local farm shop to ensure their freshness.

MAKE IT LAST! Fresh beans and peas are best stored in the fridge. If you don't plan to eat them quickly, the beans/peas and pods can be separated and frozen.

NUTRITIONAL BENEFITS: Legumes are an important source of protein. Garden peas are filled with iron, zinc, phosphorus and vitamin B6. Broad beans are a great source of iron, folate, B vitamins and fibre.

EDIBLE AND USEFUL PARTS: Beans, peas and pods.

• **A note about broad/fava beans:**
If you take prescription monoamine oxidase inhibitors then you should not eat broad beans, as well as things like banana peel, some soy-based products like soy sauce and miso, and fermented foods like sauerkraut and kimchi. If you're unsure, please seek professional medical advice.

⊡ Beans and peas

Fresh broad beans and peas can be eaten raw, steamed, stir-fried, roasted or blended into a sauce or soup. Try both raw tossed through a salad with fresh spinach, chopped fresh mint, olive oil and lemon juice, or stirred through dishes like risotto and pasta. If you grow your own or have an abundance, try pickling them with aromatics such as garlic, fresh chilli or mustard seeds.

When preparing broad beans, as well as removing the pods, people commonly peel the shells off each individual bean to only eat the tender flesh inside. The whole broad bean is, however, edible. If you do choose to peel the beans, then save the skins and pods for boiling into a broth or blending in a food processor and adding to hummus or dips.

Roasted broad beans: These are great as nibbles to share or a snack on the go. I use broad beans, but you could also use garden peas or chickpeas. Steam the broad beans for a few minutes until slightly softened. Strain and coat them in a little rapeseed/canola oil and your choice of seasoning, such as salt, pepper, garlic powder, chilli powder, cumin or smoked paprika. Spread out evenly on a tray and bake at 180°C/350°F/gas mark 4 for 20–30 minutes until crunchy and flavoursome.

⚘ Pods

When they are fresh and young, broad bean and pea pods can be enjoyed whole with their contents, like you would a mangetout or sugar snap pea (just nip off the very end). Chop them through a salad or stew or sauté them with plant butter, minced garlic, salt and pepper. If they are too tough or stringy you could boil them to make a healthy stock or purée them into a soup.

Bean or pea pod broth: Broad bean and pea pods can be added to water and simmered for 45 minutes, by themselves or with other vegetable offcuts, to create a stock. If you plan to add your peas or beans to a dish like risotto or soup, making a pod broth to cook with is a great way to add more flavour and make use of the whole legume. On pages 232–4 there's more about how to make, store and use homemade broth.

☑ My favourite ways to compleat:

Griddled or barbequed whole beans or peas: Chop off the very end and brush your whole broad beans or pea pods with a little olive oil. Season with salt and pepper. Cook for five to ten minutes over a hot barbeque or griddle pan, turning halfway, until lightly charred and softened through. Best when the broad beans or garden peas are fresh and young. Also try this with other beans and peas, such as runner beans or sugar snap peas.

Whole bean or pea pod tempura: Tempura is great made with a variety of vegetables, and you can also use broad bean and pea pods, with or without the beans/peas. To make a simple batter, sift 60g/2¼oz/scant ½ cup plain/all-purpose flour, one teaspoon baking powder and ¼ teaspoon salt into a bowl. Add extra seasoning such as a little chilli powder or ground cumin if you wish. Whisk in 100ml/3½fl oz/scant ½ cup cold water, removing any lumps. Set aside for ten minutes. When ready, heat two tablespoons of rapeseed/canola oil in a frying pan over a medium to high heat. Test if it is hot enough by dropping a bit of batter into the oil and seeing if it sizzles. Chop the very end off the bean and/or pea pods and dip them whole into the batter so that they are well coated, then carefully place them in the frying pan. Cook for a few minutes each side until crispy. Add more oil if needed. Once cooked, place on a plate with a sheet of paper towel to soak up any excess oil. Serve with sweet chilli sauce for dipping.

Compleat Recipe: Harusame-Style Shredded Broad Bean and Noodle Salad

This raw salad is inspired by Japanese harusame (glass noodle) bowls, which often incorporate shredded edamame beans. Instead, I have chosen to use tasty raw broad beans and pods. You could also try this with your choice of edible peas in pods. Make sure you choose broad beans which are fresh and young and remove any parts which are overly stringy or tough. Whilst glass noodles are traditionally used, you could opt for other vegan noodles, such as soba or wholewheat noodles.

Prep 30 minutes. **Cooking** 5 minutes
Serves 4

For the noodle salad:
- 400g/14oz fresh broad/fava beans in pods
- ½ red cabbage
- 2 carrots
- 1 head of broccoli, including stalk
- 2 nests glass or other vegan noodles
- 2 teaspoons sesame seeds

For the dressing:
- 4 tablespoons rice vinegar
- 3 tablespoons dark soy sauce
- 4 teaspoons brown sugar
- 2 tablespoons sesame oil
- 1 tablespoon neutral oil (walnut or rapeseed/canola work well)
- 2 teaspoons sriracha
- Salt and black pepper

1   Prepare the broad beans by very thinly slicing the pods and beans. These are going to be served raw, so shred them thoroughly and remove any overly stringy bits from the pods. You're aiming for a crunchy but pleasant texture.

2   Thinly slice the raw red cabbage, like you would for a coleslaw, including the cabbage heart if you wish. The carrots should be prepared into ribbons, using a peeler to create fine strips and including the skin. Chop the broccoli into small florets and finely chop the stalk into strips. Include any leaves, if your broccoli head has them.

3   Prepare the noodles according to the packet's instructions. Strain and separate into four deep bowls. Leave to cool whilst you mix the dressing.

4   In a small bowl, combine the rice vinegar, dark soy sauce, brown sugar, sesame oil, neutral oil and sriracha. Add a splash of water and mix well with a fork. Season with salt and pepper to taste.

5   Top your bowls of noodles with all of the prepared raw vegetables. Drizzle over the dressing and mix well before eating. Finish by sprinkling the sesame seeds over each dish.

▦ Green-fingered ideas

Did you know that the whole young garden pea plant is edible? It is often sold as pea shoots, but is inexpensive to grow your own. Plant pea seeds – or dried peas that have been pre-soaked for 24 hours – a couple of centimetres deep in moist compost. Water well and the shoots will be ready to harvest in two weeks. These work well in trays on your windowsill so are great to grow if you don't have much space. They are delicious raw in a salad and are an excellent source of vitamins A and C. Lesser known are broad bean shoots, which are also edible and can be grown by following the same steps. Turn to pages 239–40 for more about microgreens like these.

Broccoli

The whole broccoli head is edible, nutritious and versatile – so, go on, compleat your broccoli! Try it steamed, raw, stir-fried, roasted or added to dishes such as a Thai green curry. The stalk has always been my favourite part and I seek out the broccoli with the biggest stalk when shopping. It has a lovely crunchy texture and is delicious raw or cooked.

IN SEASON: Available year-round but at its best from August to October.

MAKE IT LAST! Broccoli is best stored in the fridge. To freshen up an old head or floret of broccoli, stand it in a glass or jar of water in the fridge. Broccoli can also be chopped, blanched and frozen to preserve it for longer.

NUTRITIONAL BENEFITS: Broccoli is full of goodness, including lots of vitamins C and K, calcium, protein and folate, as well as some vitamin A. It is a good plant-based source of alpha-linolenic acid, or ALA, an important type of omega-3 fatty acid. Broccoli also contains choline, a nutrient needed to support all cells, as well as memory development. The broccoli stalk is just as nourishing and also contains even more fibre. Include raw as well as cooked broccoli in your diet to get the most from its nutrients.

EDIBLE AND USEFUL PARTS: Florets, stalks and leaves.

✸ Florets

The florets work especially well as tempura
(page 48), tossed through pasta, or raw in a salad
with lentils, tomatoes and seeds.I prefer to eat
broccoli florets raw or lightly fried in sesame oil,
rather than boiled or steamed, as they retain mor
of their satisfying crunch. See "my favourite ways
to compleat" for more ideas.

✸ Stalk

Broccoli stalk is tasty and full of goodness. There's no need at all to peel
it – just chop it into slices or chunks. Enjoy the stalk raw in salads or as a
crudité with hummus, or cook it as you would the florets. It has a slightly
more subtle flavour, a bit like kohlrabi, and a lovely al dente texture.

Summer rolls: These traditionally Vietnamese rice rolls are a healthy starter
or main and can be filled with any raw vegetables. Broccoli stalk works
well because it is flavour-rich and easy to slice into thin batons. Slice the
stalk into strips with other raw vegetables like radish, cucumber, carrot, red
cabbage and spring onion/scallion. Wrap the vegetables, plus optional fresh
coriander/cilantro, in rehydrated rice paper sheets to create little parcels.
Serve with sweet chilli or peanut sauce for dipping.

Kimchi: Broccoli stalk is great sliced and added to kimchi for a crunchy,
spicy ferment. Turn to pages 133–5 for my recipe.

✸ Leaves

I always save any leaves from a head of broccoli. When we buy broccoli,
the leaves tend to be small and sparse. However, these are still great
added to a salad, stir-fried or used as you would other greens.

☑ My favourite ways to compleat:

Cauliflower and broccoli cheeze: Broccoli works well in a baked cauliflower cheeze. My recipe on pages 72–3 uses cauliflower and kale but is just as tasty made using a whole head of cauliflower and broccoli. You can include the stalks and leaves, as well as the florets.

Slaws with broccoli florets and/or stalk: Broccoli, especially the shredded stalk, is a great addition to a slaw. Turn to the beetroot chapter on page 37 for my raw beet, broccoli and carrot slaw. Or for a slightly more traditional coleslaw, including the broccoli stalk, turn to the cabbage chapter on pages 63–4.

Glass noodle and raw vegetable salad: I love both the broccoli stalk and florets raw in a salad – they are crisp and flavoursome. For a more unusual dish, turn to pages 49–50 to try my salad inspired by Japanese harusame (glass noodle) bowls, with broad/fava beans, cabbage, carrot, broccoli and sesame.

Stir-fried offcut greens: I love the simplicity of stir-fried greens – cook with slices of garlic and sesame oil and it's effortlessly tasty. As well as broccoli florets, you can incorporate chopped broccoli and kale stalks or other unloved greens, like cauliflower or sprout leaves, for a different take on traditional greens.

• **A note about veggie offcuts broth:** Whilst most vegetable offcuts are delicious added to a broth (pages 232–4), be aware that brassicas like broccoli can cause your broth to taste bitter so add these sparingly if at all.

Compleat Recipe: Warming Ramen Noodle Bowls with Crispy Tofu, Mushrooms and Broccoli

I love a steaming bowl of ramen, topped with sesame fried broccoli, mushrooms and tofu. I like to use homemade stock in my ramen, which you can make from leftover vegetable offcuts (see pages 232–4). It gives the ramen a rich flavour and deep colour. Press the tofu in advance, ideally the night before, or buy pre-pressed.

Prep 15 minutes. **Cooking** 45 minutes
Serves 4

- 1 tablespoon toasted sesame oil, plus 2 teaspoons for the tofu and extra if needed
- 1 red onion, diced
- 2 carrots, diced
- 4 garlic cloves, finely chopped
- 1 red chilli, finely diced
- 5cm/2in piece of root ginger, grated (no need to peel)
- ½ teaspoon ground turmeric
- 1 teaspoon ground cumin
- 2 teaspoons curry powder
- ½ teaspoon Chinese five spice powder
- 2l/70fl oz/8¾ cups stock (I use stock made from vegetable offcuts, see pages 232–4, or shop bought)

- 2¼ teaspoons light soy sauce
- 3 tablespoons miso paste
- 8 cabbage or green leaves of your choice, shredded
- 2 sheets sushi nori (optional)
- 1 small broccoli head and stalk
- 400g/14oz pack firm organic tofu, pressed in advance
- 8 chestnut/cremini mushrooms
- 2 nests soba or vegan noodles of your choice
- Salt and black pepper

To serve (your choice of):
- Handful of chopped fresh coriander/cilantro
- Sriracha sauce
- Sliced spring onion/scallion
- 2 teaspoons sesame seeds

1   In a large pan with a lid, heat the tablespoon of sesame oil. Add the onion and carrot and cook over a medium heat for a few minutes. Then add the garlic and chilli, including the chilli seeds, and the grated ginger.

2   After a few minutes, stir in the turmeric, cumin, curry powder and Chinese five spice. Allow to cook for 2 minutes then add the stock, 2 teaspoons of the soy sauce and the miso paste. Shred the cabbage leaves and add these, as well as any leaves from the broccoli head. Tear the optional nori into small pieces and add to the pan. Stir and simmer for 15 minutes over a medium to low heat with the lid on.

3 Meanwhile, prepare the tofu (ideally pressed in advance) by draining it and slicing into rectangular cubes. Slice the mushrooms and chop the broccoli stalk into similar-sized pieces. Separate the rest of the broccoli into small florets.

4 Check the broth and season with salt and pepper to taste. Once the 15 minutes have passed, turn the broth to a low heat.

5 In a large frying pan, heat 2 teaspoons sesame oil over a medium to high heat. Add the prepared tofu and drizzle over the remaining ¼ teaspoon soy sauce. The heat should remain fairly high so that the tofu fries and turns crispy on the outside, whilst being softened on the inside. Check and turn the tofu frequently so that all of the sides are evenly cooked.

6 Once the tofu is nearly cooked, add the mushrooms and broccoli, plus extra oil if needed. Cook for around 5 minutes so that the vegetables are flavoured and still a little crunchy. At the same time, add the noodles to the broth pan and allow them to simmer and cook for around 5 minutes (or as per the packet's instructions). Once everything is cooked, remove the pans from the heat.

7 Serve in large deep bowls. First, evenly ladle the broth and all of the ingredients from the saucepan into the bowls. Ensure that the noodles are evenly divided. Top the ramen with the crispy tofu, mushrooms and broccoli.

8 Add your choice of extra toppings. I like to chop over fresh coriander leaves and stems, add a few dashes of sriracha, a sprinkle of sliced spring onion and some sesame seeds to finish.

Green pet foods

My dog loves steamed broccoli. When preparing a head of broccoli, I will often steam a few small slices of the stalk for her. Once cooled, they are a lovely, nutritious treat to feed sparingly.

Brussels sprouts

I was never a fan of sprouts and would eat just a few, and only ever at Christmas. However, forget the idea that we need to trim and cut a cross at the base of each sprout, before throwing the offcuts away and boiling them to within an inch of their life! Cooked well, and often whole, sprouts are packed with taste and nutrition. The whole plant is in fact edible, including the little sprouts, large stalk they are often sold on and the lesser seen leafy top.

IN SEASON: October – March

MAKE IT LAST! Brussels sprouts are best stored in the fridge. If they're sold on the stalk, that's a sign that they're fresh – store the whole stalk in a cool, dark place or the fridge. The sprouts can also be blanched and frozen to preserve them for longer.

NUTRITIONAL BENEFITS:
Sprouts are a great source of iron, which helps red blood cells form haemoglobin to transport oxygen. They also contain manganese, phosphorus, folate, fibre and vitamins A, C and K, as well as all of the B vitamins.

EDIBLE AND USEFUL PARTS:
Whole sprouts, leaves and stalks.

▣Whole sprouts

Like mini cabbages, each sprout can be compleated whole. There's no need to remove the outer leaves or tip of each little stalk unless they are especially tatty or old. Rather than boiling, I prefer to roast or sauté, which gives the sprouts a richer, earthy taste. You could also add them to a stir-fry with vegetables or offcut greens (page 53). Also try shredding the raw leaves through a salad or coleslaw (page 63) as an alternative to cabbage.

Maple roasted swede/rutabaga and sprouts with nuts: Give sprouts and swede the attention they deserve with this subtly sweet and satisfying dish. I like to use walnuts; however, you could use any nuts of your choice. Chop one medium swede into even pieces of around 3cm/1¼in, leaving the skin on. In a bowl, coat the swede with one tablespoon rapeseed/canola oil, two teaspoons maple syrup, ¼ teaspoon dried thyme and a little salt and pepper. Mix well and tip into an ovenproof dish with four whole garlic cloves. Roast in the oven at 190°C/375°F/gas mark 5 for 30 minutes. Meanwhile, in the bowl, toss ten halved sprouts with three tablespoons chopped walnuts, one teaspoon rapeseed oil, one teaspoon maple syrup and a little salt and pepper. After the 30 minutes, add this mix to the dish with the swede and return to the oven for 10-15 minutes until it is all well-cooked, but the sprouts retain some bite.

Toasted sprouts with chestnuts: I like to forage for chestnuts in autumn and freeze them to use in dishes over winter. However, you can also buy chestnuts or use hazelnuts or walnuts as an alternative. Slice each sprout in half and chop the nuts. Sauté in a frying pan over a medium heat with a little butter for a few minutes, until slightly charred and softened but still retaining some crunch.

🖼️ Leaves

If you grow your own brussels sprouts or have ever seen the whole plant in a shop, you'll know that the round sprouts are only a small, albeit tasty, part of the plant. Sprouts grow as buds on a tall, thick stalk, topped with large green foliage, which looks very like a cabbage. These leaves are edible but can taste bitter. I suggest testing them first, choosing the young leaves where possible. These could be shredded sparingly through a stir-fry, soup, stew or ramen, or chopped and sautéed with butter, garlic, lemon juice and seasoning.

🌱 Stalk

The stalk provides brussels sprouts with their nutrients and moisture. Although tough on the outside, it is also edible. It's great roasted whole, with the sprouts attached, eaten raw or added to a stir-fry. The taste is similar to broccoli stalk! If the plant is young or small then the whole stalk may be edible, but you'll usually need to remove some of the harder skin. Once carved, the centre of the stalk is crunchy but tender and well worth compleating.

☑ My favourite ways to compleat:

Roasted whole stalk of sprouts: Many recipes roast the sprout stalk and serve it on a big platter to eat the sprouts and discard the stalk. However, the stalk itself is delicious too – albeit a little fiddly! Roasting really brings out the flavour. Place your sprout stalk (with sprouts attached) in an ovenproof dish. If required, carefully chop it in half and use two dishes. Drizzle over two to three tablespoons rapeseed/canola oil, one teaspoon balsamic vinegar and season well with salt and pepper. Use your hands to massage this all over the stalk and sprouts, ensuring it is well coated.

Add four whole garlic cloves to the dish and cook at 190°C/375°F/gas mark 5 for 40 minutes to an hour, depending on the size. Check and turn it every 20 minutes. Serve as a side or with a roast dinner. To eat, twist the sprouts off the stalk. The stalk may be too hard on the outside, but scrape out the soft centre, which is full of flavour.

• **A note about veggie offcuts broth:** Whilst most vegetable offcuts are delicious added to a broth (pages 232–4), be aware that brassicas like sprouts can cause your broth to taste bitter so add these sparingly if at all.

Compleat Recipe: Bubble and Squeak Sprout Patties

Bubble and squeak has always been a tradition in our family on Boxing Day, after a long chilly walk. These patties are inspired by those memories and can be made using leftover root vegetables and sprouts saved from a roast dinner or cooked from scratch. The sprouts are shredded, including all leaves and the little stalks. Only remove any leaves that are especially brown or tatty – most will be great to compleat.

Prep 20 minutes. **Cooking** 10 minutes, plus cooking the veg if needed
Serves 4

• 2 medium potatoes
• 1 medium parsnip
• 1 medium carrot
• 15–20 medium sprouts

• 2 spring onions/scallions, chopped
• 3 tablespoons plant butter
• ½ teaspoon garlic powder
• Salt and black pepper
• Vegan aioli (see page 87) or chutney (pages 225–6) and/or salad, to serve

1 Chop the potatoes, parsnip and carrot into small even pieces. No need to peel these. If using root vegetables leftover from a roast dinner, then skip to the next step. If using fresh, then chop and par boil these for around 10 minutes.

2 Meanwhile, shred the sprouts, including the little stalks and all leaves. In a frying pan, melt half the butter, then increase to a high heat and fry the sprouts for 3–5 minutes until just starting to brown (or until warmed if your sprouts are already cooked). Turn off the heat.

3 In a bowl, use a vegetable masher to smash the cooked potatoes, parsnip, carrot and sprouts. Aim for this to still have chunks, rather than a smooth mash. Stir through the spring onions and season with salt, pepper and the garlic powder. Add two teaspoons melted butter and mix well.

4 Divide the mix into eight patties and shape using your hands. Heat the remaining butter in the frying pan over a medium to high heat to cook the patties. Cook for a few minutes on each side until fully warmed and slightly charred and crispy on the outside. Great served with a vegan garlic mayonnaise aioli or chutney and salad.

Cabbage

Sometimes overlooked, cabbage is a versatile vegetable with many different varieties, such as the white, red and Savoy cabbages and spring greens. It is especially tasty in pickles and ferments, which are useful ways to preserve a harvest of your own cabbages. Don't forget the crunchy but tasty cabbage core!

IN SEASON: Year-round

MAKE IT LAST! Cabbage is best stored in a cool, dark place or in the fridge. Limp looking leaves can be revived by submerging them in iced water for a few minutes.

NUTRITIONAL BENEFITS: Cabbage is a great source of vitamins C and K, as well as folate, which helps produce and maintain new cells.

EDIBLE AND USEFUL PARTS: Leaves, core and stalks.

Leaves

Cabbage leaves are great raw, sautéed, steamed or shredded into salads and slaws. Also try finely chopping leaves and adding to mashed potato with garlic to make a traditional colcannon side (recipe pages 185–6).

Stuffed cabbage leaves: Cabbage leaves can be separated, blanched, chilled and stuffed with fresh vegetables, herbs and grains, much like stuffed vine leaves. On pages 73–4 I've included a recipe for stuffed cauliflower leaves with herby cauli rice. Follow the same steps with cabbage leaves and substitute the cauli rice with a grain such as rice or quinoa, if you wish.

❄ ✥ Core and stalk

The centre of a cabbage may be tougher than the leaves, but that makes it perfect for slicing into stir-fries or salads. Try pickling, fermenting or adding it to ramen, a stew or a pie.

☑ My favourite ways to compleat:

Kimchi: Cabbage is great shredded through fermented kimchi. Turn to pages 133–5 for my recipe. The cabbage leaves and core can both be sliced and added.

Pickled: Red cabbage is most often pickled, but any sliced cabbage leaves and core work well. See page 235 for my easy pickling recipe.

Ramen: This noodle soup is traditionally made with cabbage such as pak choi/bok choy. However, try using other varieties, such as Savoy. Thinly slice the leaves and add to your ramen broth or chop the cabbage core and fry in a little sesame oil before adding to your ramen. See pages 53–5 for my ramen recipe.

Sauerkraut: This fermented dish is crunchy and tangy, great as a side or topping for veggie hot dogs, burgers and salads. I'm a big fan of fermented vegetables because the process preserves the produce, enhances the taste and is great for your gut. It's important to ensure everything is clean when

fermenting (wash produce, hands and utensils before touching). This recipe makes enough to fill a one-litre/one-quart preserving jar, or two smaller jars. Thinly slice the leaves and core of one cabbage (traditionally white cabbage but try any variety). In a bowl, massage one tablespoon fine sea salt into the sliced cabbage until a natural brine forms. This should take five to ten minutes. Mix in any spices, such as one tablespoon of peppercorns, cumin seeds, caraway seeds or dried chilli flakes. Pack this into your clean jar, ensuring there are no air bubbles. Cover this with a "follower" (a couple of outer leaves from the cabbage) to seal the top. The cabbage needs to be weighed down in the jar so that it is completely submerged in the brine. To do this you can use a fermentation weight or a clean glass jar filled with water. Don't seal the sauerkraut closed, instead cover it over with a dish towel or muslin/cheese cloth, so that air can filter through but no debris, and use a rubber band or string to secure. Leave to ferment at room temperature on a shelf out of direct sunlight for seven to ten days until tangy to taste. Check daily to ensure that the cabbage is covered in the brine and press down on the weight to allow any air bubbles to escape. The longer it is left to ferment, the sharper the taste. Once ready, store in a sealed jar in the fridge.

• **A note about veggie offcuts broth:** Whilst most vegetable offcuts are delicious added to a broth (pages 232-4), be aware that brassicas like cabbage can cause your broth to taste bitter so add these sparingly if at all.

Compleat Recipe: Homemade Zero-Waste Coleslaw

Coleslaw is traditionally made with cabbage, carrot and onion but like to slice through a mix of raw vegetables. This recipe incorporates cabbage and a sliced broccoli stalk. You could also add ingredients like carrot tops, apple peel, red cabbage, cauliflower leaves and spring onion/scallion, and fresh herbs like chives, parsley and coriander/cilantro. Try serving this in a bun alongside my barbeque pulled banana peel (recipe on page 28-9).

Prep 10 minutes

Makes a generous bowl's worth

- ¼ white cabbage, plus the core (or use a cabbage of your choice)
- 1 broccoli stalk
- 2 medium carrots
- ¼ red onion
- 4 tablespoons vegan mayonnaise (see page 87 for my recipe)
- 2 teaspoons lemon juice
- Fresh herbs (optional)
- Black pepper

1 Finely shred the cabbage core and broccoli stalk and cut the cabbage leaves into thin strips. Add to a bowl and grate in the carrots without peeling. Chop the red onion into fine slices and add.

2 In a bowl, prepare the dressing by mixing the vegan mayonnaise with 2 tablespoons water and the lemon juice. Stir this through the vegetable mix. Season with a little pepper to taste and any optional fresh herbs. Serve chilled.

Carrot

Queueing at my local vegetable market one day, I noticed a bucket filled with the carrot tops people had asked the seller to remove and discard. I enquired and she gave me a huge bunch to feed as a treat to my rabbit, Izzie. In truth, the whole bunch was too much for Izzie, so I chopped the rest through salads and dishes. Taking the unwanted carrot tops home became a weekly custom. Unlike the sweet flesh, the leaves are earthy and peppery – perfect for pesto or soup.

IN SEASON: May - September

MAKE IT LAST! Carrots are best stored in the fridge and can also be chopped and frozen. If your carrots have the leafy tops attached, these can be removed and stood in a glass of water in the fridge to help them stay fresh.

NUTRITIONAL BENEFITS: Carrots are a brilliant source of vitamin A, essential for all-round health, immune function and – as the old saying goes – vision, to "help you see at night". The tops also contain vitamin C, potassium, calcium, fibre and iron.

EDIBLE AND USEFUL PARTS: Flesh, skin and leaves/tops.

🗒 🎵 Flesh and skin

I don't remember the last time I peeled a carrot. Instead, give them a good scrub and prepare as you would if the skin was removed. The skin is nutritious and just as tasty as the flesh. Roast your carrots whole, enjoy them raw grated into a salad or add to a stir-fry in ribbons. Any leftover peelings or hard ends can be used to make stock or added to a smoothie.

Peel crisps: If peeling the skins, toss them in a little oil and season with salt and pepper. Bake evenly on a tray at 180°C/350°F/gas mark 4 for five to ten minutes to create tasty crisps. For more about veggie peel crisps, see page 214-5.

Carrot "bacon": Make this from leftover peels or whole carrot ribbons and marinade using the same ingredients as my banana peel "bacon" recipe on page 28. Rather than fried, this is great wrapped around cooked vegan sausages and warmed in the oven for a few minutes, ensuring the carrot does not dry out.

Smoked "salmon" style carrot lox: Using a peeler down the length of one to two medium carrots, create carrot ribbons. Press firmly with the peeler, so that the ribbons are thin but not shavings. Alternatively, use a knife and slice very thinly. Slightly old and bendy carrots actually work especially well for the desired texture. Place the carrot ribbons in a pan of water and bring to the boil. Simmer for five minutes before straining and running under a cold tap. Set aside. Now make the marinade. In a small ovenproof dish, combine two tablespoons olive oil, four teaspoons light soy sauce, two teaspoons liquid smoke, one teaspoon of brine from a jar of capers, one teaspoon lemon juice, one sheet of crumbled sushi nori, a little black pepper and around ½ teaspoon sea salt. Add the carrot ribbons and mix well. This can be left to marinade overnight or used immediately. Once ready, cook in the oven at 170°C/325°F/gas mark 3 for 10–15 minutes. Serve with plant-based cream cheeze on toast, crackers or bagels. Top with a squeeze of lemon juice and a few capers and an optional sprinkling of chopped carrot top leaves. Also try serving this as part of my "veg royale" brunch recipe on pages 16–17.

🖉 Leaves/tops

Carrot tops are peppery and savoury in taste compared with the root. You could liken the taste to fresh parsley and use the leaves as an alternative in dishes like puttanesca, tabbouleh or as a garnish. Chop through salads and add to soups, pesto and vinaigrettes.

Carrot top pesto: In a food processor, blitz 70g/2½oz carrot tops with 10g/1/3oz fresh basil (stalks and leaves of both), plus one chopped garlic clove (add the skin too), three tablespoons chopped walnuts (or use nuts of your choice or try seeds like pine nuts or sunflower seeds), two tablespoons lemon juice, three tablespoons nutritional yeast, ¼ teaspoon salt, three tablespoons olive oil and one tablespoon water. Blend until the desired consistency is achieved. Makes enough for a small jar – ideal for two people with pasta or to use as a topping for crackers, pastry or salads. Store in a jar in the fridge for a few days. This is also ideal for freezing in portions to defrost and stir through pasta.

🖳 Odds and ends

Offcuts broth: Along with other vegetable scraps, freeze any hard carrot ends in a tub and save to make stock (see my recipe on page 232-4). You could also include the peels.

Kimchi: Carrot ends and offcuts, as well as whole carrot slices, are great fermented in kimchi. Find my recipe on pages 133–5.

☑ My favourite ways to compleat:

Cabbage heart and carrot coleslaw: Try incorporating some of the shredded leaves and carrot into a coleslaw. You can also add things like chopped cabbage heart and broccoli stalk or shredded cauliflower leaves. See pages 63–4 for my recipe. Carrot also works well in a grated beetroot slaw, see page 37 for that recipe.

Compleat carrot and potato soup: This soup includes carrot tops and was inspired by a wartime recipe broadcast by the Kitchen Front, encouraging people to make their produce go further. In a large saucepan, heat a knob of plant butter. Sauté one diced white onion and two minced garlic cloves for a few minutes (save the onion and garlic skins for making stock, page 232–4). Add one chopped medium potato and 300g/10½oz chopped carrots. No need to peel these. After a few minutes, add 700ml/24fl oz/3 cups stock. Stock can be shop bought or homemade veggie offcuts broth (pages 232–4). Season, and if using homemade stock, be generous with the salt. Simmer for ten minutes, then add a bunch of chopped carrot tops (roughly 30g/1oz worth), using both the stalks and leaves. Simmer for a further 15 minutes. Add ½ teaspoon dried thyme. Stir and remove from the heat and blend using a hand blender. Garnish with a few carrot top leaves.

Compleat Recipe: Carrot Top Tabbouleh

Tabbouleh is traditionally made with fresh parsley and mint. But carrot tops are a tasty alternative. This recipe combines them with bulgur wheat, raw vegetables and nuts. If you don't have the exact ingredients to hand, use any fresh vegetables you wish and swap the bulgur for a different grain, like pearl barley or couscous.

Prep 35 mins

Serves 2 as a main, or a group to share as a side

- 200g/7oz/scant 1¼ cups bulgur wheat
- 450ml/16fl oz/scant 2 cups boiling water, with a little vegetable stock powder/bouillon
- 50g/1¾oz chopped nuts of your choice (hazelnuts and Brazil nuts work well)

- 1 teaspoon cumin seeds
- 2-3 carrots (roughly 75g/2½oz), diced
- Bunch of carrot tops (roughly 50g/1¾oz), finely chopped
- 1 large tomato, chopped
- ½ medium cucumber, diced
- 1 spring onion/scallion, sliced
- 1 tablespoon olive oil
- 1 tablespoon lemon juice
- Salt and black pepper

1　Prepare the bulgur wheat by soaking it in a bowl in the boiling water with the bouillon stirred through for 20-30 minutes until the water is absorbed. Fluff the grains with a fork, check it is ready and strain if needed.

2　In a pan, toast the chopped nuts with the cumin seeds over a low heat for 2-3 minutes until aromatic but not burned.

3　Once the bulgur is ready, combine with the chopped vegetables, carrot tops, nuts and seeds in a bowl. Add the olive oil and lemon juice. Mix well and season to taste. Serve chilled as a main, side or part of a meze.

🌱 Green-fingered ideas

If you've ever left a carrot for too long before cooking it you may have noticed the top begin to sprout new leaves. You can also achieve this by saving a 2cm/¾in piece of the top of a carrot. Rest it in a saucer with a little water on your windowsill for around a week and green leaves should begin to sprout from the top, forming new carrot tops for you to harvest and enjoy. Change the water regularly and be careful not to let it get mouldy.

Cauliflower

I love cauliflower and have been known to come home from dinner at a friend's house with a bag of unwanted cauli leaves. Like the cauliflower head, the leaves are tasty, nutritious and versatile. As well as the well-known white cauliflower, there are other colourful varieties and the beautiful Romanesco cauliflower, native to Italy. Cauliflower is delicious roasted, fermented, raw or blended into sauces.

IN SEASON: January – April

MAKE IT LAST! Cauliflower is best stored in the fridge. To freshen up an old cauliflower, stand it in a glass or jar of water in the fridge. Cauliflower can be chopped, blanched and frozen to preserve it for longer.

NUTRITIONAL BENEFITS: Cauliflower is really high in vitamin C, which has many roles, including boosting immunity and helping with the absorption of iron. It is a good source of vitamin K and folate. Like other greens, the leaves are especially nutrition-packed.

Cauliflowers were named as part of the "clean 15" in recent research. This means that they were found to contain little, if any, pesticide residues!

EDIBLE AND USEFUL PARTS: Florets, stalks and leaves.

❇️🥬 Florets and stalk

Cauliflower has become a regular on vegan menus because its flesh absorbs flavour, making it ideal for baking whole, adding to curries or chopping and baking as "steaks" or "wings".

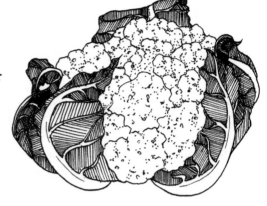

Cauliflower alfredo pasta: Chop the stalk and florets of a medium cauliflower and boil for seven to ten minutes until softened. Strain and purée the cooked cauliflower in a blender with 250ml/9fl oz/1 cup plant milk, two tablespoons plant butter, two whole cloves garlic (skin on) and salt and pepper to taste until smooth. Serve stirred through cooked pasta, such as tagliatelle or spaghetti, with garden peas.

Cauli rice: This is great for stuffing cauliflower leaves (recipe on pages 73–4), using as an alternative to rice in sushi or including in salads, such as tabbouleh. Chop your raw cauliflower florets and stalk into even pieces and blitz in a food processor to form a rice. This can be used as is, but I like to blitz in a handful of fresh parsley and mint, the zest and juice of half a lemon, one tablespoon of olive oil, a little chopped onion and seasoning. Tasty and light.

🌿 Leaves

Cauliflower leaves are tasty and versatile. Use them as you would other greens – raw, stir-fried or mixed into curries and soups. I like to sauté them with garlic and serve as a side or chopped through mashed potato to create a colcannon-style dish, recipe on pages 185–6.

Salad: All parts of a cauliflower are delicious raw and add a nutty crunch to salads. Shred the leaves through a salad in place of greens or use in a coleslaw (recipe pages 63–4).

☑ My favourite ways to compleat:

Stir-fry: The leaves, chopped stalk and florets can all be added to a stir-fry along with other vegetables. The leaves are especially tasty with a clove of chopped garlic and chilli to taste.

Kimchi or pickle: Cauliflower leaves, stalk and florets are all delicious pickled or fermented in kimchi. Find my recipes on pages 133–5 and 235.

Roasted whole: The texture of cauliflower is beautiful when roasted. You only need to remove any old or very large leaves. These can be sautéed and served on the side. Preheat the oven to 190°C/375°F/gas mark 5 and place the cauliflower in an ovenproof dish. Drizzle generously with olive oil and season. Sprinkle over your choice of seasoning, such as sumac, ground cumin, smoked paprika or garlic powder. Roast for 45 minutes to an hour until soft in the centre. Tasty served with fresh herbs, like parsley and mint, chopped over the top and a squeeze of lemon juice.

Compleat cauliflower cheeze: This plant-based take on a classic cauliflower cheese is waste-free and full of flavour. Soak 200g/7oz cashews in a bowl of water in advance of making this – overnight is ideal but at least 30 minutes. Prepare one small cauliflower. First, remove the leaves and set aside. Chop the florets and stalk into equal sized pieces of around 5cm/2in. Bring a saucepan of water to the boil, add the florets and stalk and simmer for seven to ten minutes until softened but not overdone. Drain and place in an ovenproof dish with the roughly chopped cauliflower leaves and 50g/2oz chopped kale, including stalks. To make the sauce, drain the cashews and place in a blender with 260ml/9½fl oz/generous 1 cup plant milk, four tablespoons nutritional yeast, two whole garlic cloves, skin left on, 1½ teaspoons smoked paprika, one teaspoon English mustard, ½ teaspoon salt and pepper to taste. Blend until smooth, pour into the dish and mix well, ensuring everything is coated. Sprinkle over a little nutritional yeast. Bake in the oven at 190°C/375°F/gas mark 5 for 20 minutes until lightly golden on top.

Compleat Recipe: Stuffed Cauliflower Leaves with Herby Cauli Rice

I was inspired by stuffed vine leaves when creating this recipe, which makes the most of the whole cauliflower. The leaves are filled with raw cauli rice, complemented by zesty herbs. These are light, refreshing and really tasty. I recommend serving as a starter, side or as part of a meze with hummus, salad and fermented vegetables or pickles.

Prep 30 minutes **Cooking** 1 minute
Makes roughly 10 stuffed leaf parcels

- 1 whole cauliflower
- Handful of fresh mint
- Handful of fresh parsley
- Zest and juice of ½ lemon
- 1 large tomato, diced
- 1 whole spring onion/scallion, chopped
- ½ teaspoon dried chilli flakes
- 1 tablespoon olive oil
- Salt and black pepper

1   Prepare the cauliflower by first removing the leaves – these are going to be your wraps. Cut out any thick stalks from the centre of the leaves and reserve. Smaller leaves can be left whole. Blanch the leaves by immersing them in a pan of boiled water for 30 seconds. Strain and place the leaves in a bowl of iced water for 30 seconds, then strain and set aside.

2   Now prepare the cauli rice by separating the cauliflower florets and chopping the stalk. Place these in a food processor with the mint, parsley, lemon zest and juice. Season generously and blitz until rice-like. Place the cauli rice in a bowl with the diced tomato, chopped spring onion, a few of the stalks removed previously from the leaves, diced, the chilli flakes and olive oil. Mix well.

3   Now stuff the leaves. To do this, choose leaves the size of your hand or layer smaller leaves to create hand-sized wraps. Lay the leaves flat and spoon 2–3 teaspoons of the cauli rice in a rectangle in the centre of each wrap, being careful not to overfill. Fold in the ends of each wrap and roll into a sausage shape. Serve cold as part of a meze. Save any leftover cauli rice to use in salads or as a side. Any leftover stalks from leaves can be sautéed or chopped through salad.

Celeriac/celery root

I love this often overlooked, nonconformist root vegetable. Don't be put off by its appearance, the whole celeriac can be eaten. It is delicious, with a slightly sweet and nutty flavour. Great roasted and mashed, or added to soups, pies and gratin.

IN SEASON: September – April

MAKE IT LAST! Celeriac is best stored in a cool, dark place or the fridge.

NUTRITIONAL BENEFITS: Celeriac is a great source of folate, potassium, fibre and vitamins C and K. Like many vegetables, much of the celeriac's nutrients are found in and close to the skin.

EDIBLE AND USEFUL PARTS: Flesh, skin, stalks and leaves.

Flesh

With its distinctive flavour, celeriac is delicious roasted, blended into soup or boiled and mashed. Use it as you would other root vegetables and enjoy the flesh with the skin on. Rinse it well and only remove the toughest or overly blemished parts before cooking. Don't be put off by the coiled roots – once washed, these are just as tasty and can happily be eaten.

Roasted celeriac or celeriac chips: Simple but really tasty, celeriac can be chopped into chunks or chip wedges, with the skin left on, and coated in a little rapeseed/canola oil and seasoning to make chips or a delicious accompaniment for other roasted vegetables. Cook in an ovenproof dish for around 40 minutes at 180°C/350°F/gas mark 4.

Celeriac slaw: Celeriac can be eaten raw and has a real punch to its flavour. Try shredding it through a coleslaw with carrot, apple and cabbage. See pages 63-4 for my coleslaw recipe. Great with some lemon juice and chopped parsley, or chopped celeriac leaves, if you have them.

Celeriac, leek and potato soup: This tasty soup uses a whole skin-on celeriac with potato, leek and homemade stock. It's topped with the shredded and sautéed green leek top that we often throw away. See the leek chapter (pages 153-4) for the recipe.

Skin

I wince when I read recipes that tell you to remove the celeriac skin and chop off a huge wedge at each end. This is all edible, especially when making soup or roasted celeriac. However, if you do remove the peel then transform it into a tasty dish.

Peel crisps: Peel the skins, toss them in a little oil and season with salt, pepper and a little garlic powder. Bake evenly on a tray at 180°C/350°F/ gas mark 4 for eight to ten minutes to create tasty crisps, great for topping soup or sharing. For more about veggie peel crisps, see pages 214-5.

Leaves

Unfortunately it's rare to find celeriac sold with the leaves or stalks intact. However, this root vegetable's foliage is wonderfully fragrant and beautifully green in colour. The leaves taste a bit like celery and can be used in broths, stews, salads and pesto or sautéed with garlic and plant butter.

▣ Odds and ends

Offcuts broth: Along with other vegetable scraps, freeze any celeriac offcuts in a tub and save to make stock (see my recipe on page 232). You could also include the peels.

Kimchi or pickled: Whole sliced celeriac or ends and offcuts are great fermented in kimchi. You could also include any chopped leaves and stalks. Find my kimchi recipe on pages 133–5. Celeriac isn't often pickled but can be thinly sliced and preserved. It works well pickled alongside a few slices of beetroot. See page 235 for my easy pickling recipe.

Compleat Recipe: Celeriac and Potato Creamy Gratin

Flavoursome and comforting, this gratin is the perfect dish for a cold afternoon. It uses a whole skin-on celeriac and potato, but you could add in or substitute with other skin-on root vegetables, like parsnip, swede/rutabaga, more potato or even beetroot.

Prep 20 minutes **Cooking** 1 hour
Serves 2 as a main or 4 as a side

- 1 medium celeriac (around 500g/1lb 2oz)
- 1 medium potato (around 200g/7oz)
- 1 small white onion
- 3 garlic cloves
- 300ml/10½fl oz/1¼ cups plant-based cream
- 300ml/10½fl oz/1¼ cups stock (or my homemade veggie offcuts broth recipe, see pages 232–4)
- ½ teaspoon dried thyme
- Salt and black pepper
- Greens and vegan sausages, to serve

1   Slice the celeriac and potato into thin, even slices, leaving the skin on. Thinly slice the onion and garlic cloves. (Save the onion and garlic skins for making a veggie offcuts broth if you wish, pages 232-4.)

2   In a pan, combine the cream and stock over a low to medium heat so that the liquids warm and mix well. Season generously with salt and pepper to taste and stir in the thyme. Remove from the heat.

3   Preheat the oven to 180°C/350°F/gas mark 4. In a large ovenproof dish, layer the vegetables. I suggest a base layer of celeriac, followed by a couple of layers of potato and celeriac, topped with a layer of celeriac, scattering a few onion and garlic slices between each layer.

4   Pour over the creamy broth so that it covers all of the vegetables. Bake in the oven for 1 hour, checking halfway and covering with a sheet of aluminium foil at this point. Serve hot with a side of greens and vegan sausages.

Celery

I have to admit, I disliked celery ever since a stringy stalk pulled out my wobbly tooth as a child! However, I have since conquered my fear – all in the name of compleating – and discovered that all parts of the celery plant are, in fact, rather delicious. Use the stalks as an aromatic, like you would onion, to add to soups, stews, chillies and curries. Crunchy and fragrant when raw, celery is great sliced through a salad or as crudités for dipping into homemade hummus (pages 84–5). The leafy tops are also edible and can be cooked or used as a garnish. Not to be confused with celeriac/celery root (pages 75–78).

IN SEASON: July – February

MAKE IT LAST! Celery is best stored in the fridge. To reawaken limp celery, stand it in a jar of water in the fridge.

NUTRITIONAL BENEFITS: Celery has a high water content but is also a good source of fibre. It contains some potassium and calcium, as well as folate and vitamin K, which is important in helping blood to clot.

EDIBLE AND USEFUL PARTS: Stalks and leaves.

⚘ Stalks

The whole celery head is edible. Outer stalks might be a bit stringier, so are better suited to cooking into soups and stews, where there's no need to remove anything. The root base of the stalks can also be cooked into dishes like these. The inner stalks tend to be smaller and more delicate, so choose those to enjoy raw in salads. As a guide, taste test the stalks and if they are crisp to bite then there's no need to discard anything.

Celery and walnut salad: To make a simple yet tasty salad, slice a few stalks of raw celery. Break a handful of walnuts into small pieces and mix with the celery in a bowl. Chop through some celery leaves, if you wish. Drizzle it all with olive oil, mix well and season with salt and pepper to taste. Enjoy as is or add slices of tomato and/or apple, or chunks of roasted sweet potato.

⧉ Leafy tops

Celery can be sold with plentiful or sparse leafy tops. These are flavoursome and can be cooked into dishes along with the stalks or enjoyed raw. Use them as a garnish for soups and salads or blend them into a juice or smoothie. If you have abundant celery tops, try making a celery leaf pesto.

Celery leaf pesto: Celery leaves can be used to make a homemade pesto. Chop a few into your pesto alongside spinach and other greens. Or for a peppery pesto, use just the celery leaves. Find my pesto recipe on page 158 and experiment with these and the leaves from other vegetable tops, such as carrots and turnips.

☑ My favourite ways to compleat:

Pickled celery: Celery can be sliced into small chunks and pickled. It works well with your choice of peppercorns, mustard seeds and chilli flakes. The leaves can be saved or added to the jar as a garnish. Find my easy pickling recipe on page 235.

Whole braised celery: Remove and reserve the leafy tops. Slice the celery heads into quarters lengthways and place in a large ovenproof dish. Sprinkle over the chopped leaves, plus any fresh herbs of your choice, such as thyme or parsley, and two chopped garlic cloves. Drizzle over a little olive oil and season with salt and pepper. Pour over enough stock to cover the stalks. Cover with a lid or aluminium foil and bake in the oven at 180°C/350°F/gas mark 4 for 40 minutes to one hour until the celery is tender.

Compleat Recipe: Mediterranean Celery Stew

This stew is rich and comforting with the delicious flavours of celery, olives, garlic and tomatoes. Try it and you'll never think of celery as bland again! Serve warm in bowls, topped with a few of the peppery celery leaves. A hearty plant-based main, this could also be served as part of a tapas selection to share.

Prep 20 minutes. **Cooking** 50 minutes
Serves 4

- 2 celery stalks
- 1 tablespoon oil from a jar of sundried tomatoes (or homemade semi-dried tomatoes, page 223)
- 3 garlic cloves, finely chopped
- 1 small courgette/zucchini, chopped
- 1 red (bell) pepper, chopped
- ½ teaspoon dried mixed herbs
- 1 teaspoon smoked paprika
- 4 tablespoons green pitted olives, roughly chopped
- 4 sundried tomatoes (or homemade semi-dried tomatoes, page 223), roughly chopped
- 2 x 400g/14oz cans chopped tomatoes (or make your own, recipe page 222)
- 400g/14oz can butterbeans
- Handful of fresh oregano
- Salt and black pepper
- Cooked grains or garlic bread, to serve

1   Thinly slice the celery stalks (use the entire stalk, but reserve the leaves) and heat the oil over a medium to low heat in a large saucepan. Add the celery and cook for a few minutes. Add the garlic and cook for a further 2 minutes.

2   Add the courgette and red pepper and stir in, then add the mixed herbs and smoked paprika. Add the olives and sundried tomatoes and allow to cook for 2 minutes.

3   Add the chopped tomatoes and drain and add the butterbeans. (The liquid from the can of butterbeans can be saved in a jar in the fridge if you wish. It can be used in the same way as aquafaba from a can of chickpeas! See pages 86–88.) Stir well, cover with a lid and allow to simmer and cook for 20 minutes.

4   Roughly chop the fresh oregano. You can use the leaves, small stalks and any flowers. After the 20 minutes, stir these into the dish. Season with salt and pepper to taste.

5   Cover and allow to cook for a further 10–20 minutes until softened and slightly reduced. Serve in bowls with optional cooked grains or garlic bread as a side. If your celery stalks had leafy tops, chop and use as a garnish.

Green-fingered ideas

Offcuts from the base of a head of celery can be used to regrow some celery stalks. To do so, save a 2cm/¾in piece from the root end of your celery head. Rest it in a saucer with a little water, using cocktail sticks to stand it upright if needed. Place on your windowsill and it will soon begin to grow new stalks out of the top of the offcut. Change the water regularly and be careful not to let it get mouldy. The stalks can be harvested and eaten as normal. Take care and they will regrow time and time again. If your plant becomes well established, it can be transferred to a pot with compost to allow it to grow further.

Chickpeas/garbanzo beans and aquafaba

The wonder ingredient of plant-based cooking, chickpeas brought us the vegan staples of hummus and falafels, and now ... aquafaba. Both the legume and the liquid are really versatile and a great go-to to add goodness to a dish. Chickpea/gram/garbanzo flour is made from dried ground chickpeas. It is a good gluten-free flour option and is widely used in plant-based cooking – great for making things like a vegan "omelette" (pages 116–17), quiche or frittata.

IN SEASON: Chickpeas are available year-round and are usually grown in warm climates like Asia. However, they can be grown in the UK and are beginning to be introduced to farms with a summer harvesting period.

MAKE IT LAST! Chickpeas are usually sold in a can or dried. These should be stored airtight at room temperature. Fresh chickpeas should be kept in the fridge.

Aquafaba can be stored in a jar in the fridge for a couple of days or frozen for two months. Try freezing it in an ice cube tray and measure one teaspoon into each hole, ready to defrost and use as required.

NUTRITIONAL BENEFITS: Chickpeas are an excellent source of protein, as well as iron, zinc and vitamin B6, important for red blood cell metabolism and stabilizing blood sugar levels. Aquafaba also contains a little protein.

EDIBLE AND USEFUL PARTS: Chickpeas/garbanzo beans, aquafaba liquid, whole pods.

⊡ Chickpeas/garbanzo beans

Chickpeas are great for adding goodness and flavour to any dish – delicious in a salad, soup, tagine or curry. Try my coconutty kale and chickpea dahl recipe on page 146.

Homemade falafels: My falafel recipe on pages 15-16 incorporates the offcut ends from a bunch of asparagus with chickpeas, fresh herbs and some spices. These are really tasty, but equally, you can make the falafels and omit the asparagus if you don't have it to hand. Homemade falafels have an amazing texture and taste nothing like the dry ones you can find in a supermarket - more than worth making from scratch.

Roasted chickpeas: These are great as a snack or an alternative to crisps. Place cooked chickpeas in a bowl and coat them in a little rapeseed/canola oil and your choice of seasoning, such as salt, pepper, garlic powder, chilli powder, cumin or smoked paprika. Bake evenly on a tray at 180°C/350°F/ gas mark 4 for around 30 minutes until crunchy and flavoursome.

Hummus with all the extras: This simple recipe can be customized to add toppings and seasonings of your choice. To make a basic hummus, drain a 400g/14oz can of chickpeas (save the aquafaba). Place the chickpeas in a food processor with one garlic clove, one tablespoon tahini and two tablespoons lemon juice. Blitz well and then taste to check if it has reached your desired consistency. For a smoother hummus, add one tablespoon at a time of aquafaba or water until you are happy. Enjoy the hummus as is or use it as a base to blend in other flavours. Store in a jar in the fridge and eat within a few days. Great served as a selection of rainbow hummus dips at a party. Try these:

Jazz Up Your Hummus

• **Harissa hummus:** I love adding a few tablespoons of homemade roasted red pepper and chilli harissa (recipe on page 95) for a lightly spiced red hummus.

• **Preserved lemon hummus:** Another favourite in our house, you can buy preserved lemons in a jar or make your own (pages 101–2). Blend in half a homemade preserved lemon, or one whole shop-bought preserved lemon, to taste, and omit the lemon juice from the base hummus.

• **Roasted beetroot hummus:** For an earthy purple hummus, blend in a roasted whole beetroot or two - delicious.

• **Roasted butternut squash or pumpkin hummus:** Blend in a few chunks of roasted, skin-on squash or pumpkin for a tasty, autumnal dip.

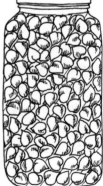

• **Green pesto topped hummus:** Try one of my pesto recipes (pages 67 and 158) and swirl this over the top of your hummus, then sprinkle over some pine nuts and drizzle with a little olive oil.

• **Roasted chickpea topped hummus:** Roast chickpeas with your choice of seasonings, such as smoked paprika (see page 84). Scatter these over the top of your hummus when serving.

• **Roasted seeds and infused oils:** Hummus is delicious served with seeds sprinkled over the top. For example, sunflower seeds or roasted pumpkin seeds (page 193). Finish with a drizzle of homemade infused oil (pages 236–7), such as chilli oil, basil oil or garlic oil.

🥛 Aquafaba

Aquafaba, or bean water, is the magical liquid found in a can of chickpeas. It is incredibly versatile and useful in a vegan kitchen. Use it as an alternative to whipped egg whites in dishes like meringue, mousse and marshmallows. It is also a reliable replacement for eggs when baking, such as my whole orange cake recipe on pages 102–3 or brownies.

How to make aquafaba: A can of unsalted chickpeas has readymade aquafaba. Just drain the can and save the liquid (use the chickpeas for another dish). Whilst chickpeas are most commonly chosen, the liquid from a can of any legumes can be used. It's best to choose the aquafaba from white beans though, such as butterbeans or haricot/navy beans, because of its consistency and colour.

You can also make aquafaba from dried chickpeas and legumes. Leave them to soak in water overnight, then simmer over a medium heat in the same water for about an hour (or as stated on the packet) until cooked. Strain the water from the chickpeas and voilà, you have aquafaba. If the liquid does not have the same consistency as from a can, simmer it on the hob for a little longer to reduce and thicken.

Aquafaba for baking: Aquafaba can be incorporated into your favourite cake and brownie recipes. As a general rule when baking, three tablespoons of aquafaba equate to one whole egg, two tablespoons of aquafaba equate to one egg white, and one tablespoon of aquafaba equates to one egg yolk. Turn to my whole orange cake recipe on pages 102–3 for an example.

Chocolate mousse: Aquafaba gives a mousse a light and fluffy finish. Melt 100g/3½oz dark vegan chocolate and set aside to cool. Meanwhile, in a bowl use an electric whisk to whip 100ml/3½fl oz/scant ½ cup aquafaba. Whisk for around ten minutes until stiff peaks form. The change really is amazing! Fold in the cooled melted chocolate to combine. Taste the mousse and add sweetener, such as agave or maple syrup, to taste. Decant into ramekins and chill for a few hours before serving. Top with optional nuts or berries.

Mayonnaise, aioli or chilli mayo: This mayonnaise is creamy and made with natural plant-based ingredients. Prepare it in a tall bowl, such as the cup from a blender, to prevent spillages. Pour in three tablespoons aquafaba, two tablespoons apple cider or white wine vinegar, two teaspoons Dijon mustard and ½ teaspoon salt. Mix with an immersion blender (a jug or cup blender won't achieve the right results). Once combined, and while still blending, pour in 250ml/9fl oz/1 cup of light-coloured neutral oil, such as sunflower or vegetable oil. (Rapeseed/canola oil works but will give the mayonnaise a yellow colour.) The sauce will quickly thicken as you blend. Transfer to a jar and store in the fridge for up to three weeks. For spicy mayonnaise, add a little harissa (page 95), sriracha or chipotle sauce to taste when blending. To make a garlic mayonnaise, or aioli, squeeze in a little lemon juice and add one to two garlic cloves when you blend the aquafaba.

Garlic and herb butter: Nina from PlantePusherne.dk discovered that aquafaba can be made into plant-based butter with a light, spreadable consistency. Truly amazing! Inspired by this recipe, my garlic and herb butter is rich and creamy – great for spreading on crackers, warm bread or enjoying with dough balls. First, melt refined/flavourless coconut oil to give you 90ml/3fl oz/1/3 cup once melted and set aside to cool. Pour four tablespoons aquafaba, ½ teaspoon apple cider vinegar and ¼ teaspoon salt into a tall cup. Once cooled, pour the coconut oil into a jug and mix with four teaspoons olive oil and one teaspoon herb oil of your choice, such as rosemary or basil oil. Using a hand blender, blend the aquafaba mix for around 30 seconds until foamy. Now place the cup on a bag of frozen vegetables or ice to help speed up the process. Continue to blend and gradually pour in the oils from the jug. After a few minutes of blending, the mixture should begin to thicken. Once this happens, add ¼ teaspoon garlic powder and ¼ teaspoon mixed herbs. Blend briefly to mix. Place this uncovered in the fridge overnight to thicken and set. Enjoy within one week.

Roasted Butternut Squash Ravioli

You can't beat fresh pasta. Filled with roasted butternut squash, this ravioli is deliciously creamy and satisfying – and it's simpler to prepare than you might think. In place of the eggs traditionally found in fresh pasta, I use aquafaba to create a dough that is pleasing and easy to work with.

Prep 30 minutes **Cooking** 50 minutes
Serves 4

For the filling:
- 500g/1lb 2oz butternut squash
- 4 garlic cloves
- Handful of fresh sage or 1 teaspoon dried sage
- 1 tablespoon rapeseed/canola oil
- Salt and black pepper

For the dough:
- 260g/9oz/2 cups plain/all-purpose flour, plus extra for dusting
- 1 teaspoon salt
- 150ml/5fl oz/scant 2/3 cup aquafaba
- 1 teaspoon olive oil

To serve:
- Your choice of oil
- Toasted pine nuts, sundried tomatoes or olives (all optional)

1   Prepare the butternut squash by removing the seeds (save if you wish) and chopping the flesh into small chunks. You can leave the skin on or remove. Place the squash in an ovenproof dish with the garlic cloves and sage. Coat in the oil and season with salt and pepper. Mix well and roast in the oven at 180°C/350°F/gas mark 4 for 30–40 minutes until roasted and softened. Set aside to cool.

2   Whilst the squash is roasting, prepare the dough. In a bowl, combine the flour and salt using a hand whisk. Pour in the aquafaba and olive oil. Knead for 5 minutes to form a ball of dough. Add a little more flour or aquafaba if needed. The dough should be smooth and not too sticky. Cover the bowl with a damp kitchen towel to prevent the dough from drying out. Set aside for 30 minutes.

3   In a food processor, blend the cooled roasted squash ingredients to a fairly smooth consistency with small chunks.

4   Flour your worktop, a rolling pin and the dough. Roll the dough out as thinly as possible to just a few millimetres thick. Using a small round cookie cutter or a glass, cut the dough into rounds. To fill the ravioli, place a round of dough in the palm of your hand and place 1–2 teaspoons of the filling in the centre. Have a bowl with a little water to hand. Run a wet finger around the edge of the dough and place another round of dough on top. To seal, pinch around the edges.

5   Repeat until you have used all of the dough, rerolling any offcuts. Any excess dough which is too small to make a ravioli parcel from can be rolled into little sausage shapes and cooked with the ravioli as pasta pieces.

6   Bring a large pan of lightly salted water to the boil and allow to simmer. Carefully drop the ravioli into the water. Don't overcrowd the pan and allow space for the pasta to move around. You might need to cook in a few batches, depending on the size of your pan.

7   After around 5 minutes, the ravioli is ready. It should float to the top of the water. Using a slotted spoon, carefully remove the ravioli from the pan. Serve in bowls, drizzled with your choice of oil and extra toppings.

⊡ Fresh chickpeas in pods

These are slowly becoming available in farm shops and markets. If you can't wait, try growing your own! When young, the pods can be eaten whole, steamed or in salads. Once mature, they can be shredded and eaten or podded to retrieve the chickpeas. The fresh chickpeas can be tossed through salads, sautéed, added to curries and other dishes or used to make a green hummus. Turn to the broad/fava bean chapter (pages 46–50) for more ideas for how to use pea pods – such as grilled whole, simmered into a broth or tempura.

⊞ Green-fingered ideas

We don't commonly see them, but that doesn't mean that chickpeas can't be grown in your garden or allotment. They can be sown from pre-soaked dried chickpeas or seeds in spring. Over summer, enjoy the young pods whole or allow them to mature to larger chickpeas.

Chillies and peppers

Despite being from the same family, peppers and chillies vary greatly in taste – from sweet to spicy. Green bell peppers are actually the unripe fruit, whilst yellow, orange and red bell peppers have each been left for longer on the plant. Also try different varieties on the heat scale of peppers and chillies, such as the super sweet pimento peppers (eaten whole, except for the stalks), the pleasantly hot serrano peppers, or the popular spicy chilli of choice, jalapeños.

IN SEASON: Chillies are available year-round but are usually grown overseas in hot climates. Bell peppers are in season from May to September.

MAKE IT LAST! Chillies and peppers are best stored in the fridge. Preserve any chillies which are leftover or past their best by freezing them whole. You can grate or carefully slice them straight from frozen into dishes. If you grow your own chillies, consider drying them out to have a stock for months to come.

NUTRITIONAL BENEFITS: Chillies and peppers are a good source of vitamins A, B6 and C. They also provide antioxidants and minerals like iron, potassium, copper and manganese. Try to incorporate raw, as well as cooked, bell peppers into your diet to get the most of their immunity-boosting vitamin C.

EDIBLE AND USEFUL PARTS:
Flesh, skin, seeds and stalks.

▣ Flesh

Whilst bell and other
sweet peppers are tasty
raw as well as cooked,
spicier chillies are
best cooked. Try bell
peppers stuffed with
grains and baked in the
oven, chopped raw through spicy rice or roasted and added to dishes.
Chillies, however, are an aromatic and are best diced to impart flavour
when cooked.

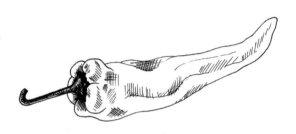

Jalapeño poppers: When I was vegetarian, these were one of my favourite junk food treats. Homemade with plant-based cream cheeze, they are just as tasty. You'll need six fresh jalapeños or mild chillies of your choice. Remove the stalks and slice the chillies in half lengthways. If you're especially brave you could leave the seeds in, but I remove them. Fill each chilli half with one tablespoon of plant-based cream cheeze. These can then be topped with breadcrumbs and baked in the oven at 180°C/350°F/gas mark 4 for 10–15 minutes or fried. For the frying method, make a buttermilk by combining 80ml/2½fl oz/1/3 cup soya milk with 1½ teaspoons lemon juice and two tablespoons soya yogurt. Mix with a fork and let rest for ten minutes so that it curdles and goes a bit frothy. Once ready, dip the prepared chillies in the buttermilk and then roll in breadcrumbs to coat. Heat 100ml/3½fl oz/scant ½ cup of rapeseed/canola oil in a frying pan over a medium to high heat. Test it is hot enough by dropping a breadcrumb into the oil and seeing if it sizzles. Once hot, carefully fry the coated chillies for a few minutes each side until crispy. Place on a plate with a sheet of paper towel to soak up any excess oil. Great served with barbeque sauce for dipping.

Roasted bell peppers: Quarter the flesh of your red or orange bell peppers and place on a baking tray with a little olive oil. Roast in the oven at 180°C/350°F/gas mark 4 for 10-15 minutes until the flesh is softened and the skin starts to blister. These are tasty as a side but even better puréed into hummus (pages 84-5) or pesto (pags 67 and 158) to transform them with a roasted red pepper flavour. Your peppers could also be roasted alongside tomatoes, onion, garlic and fresh herbs to create a rich and flavour-filled sauce for pasta and cooking (pages 222) or blended with a little coconut milk and stock to make a roasted pepper soup.

⬚ Seeds

The seeds are the hottest part of chillies, so we often scrape them out before cooking. However, they can be saved or added to dishes to give extra heat and flavour. Bell pepper seeds are also edible but aren't particularly palatable. I recommend composting or planting those unless you are making a dish where the pepper will be puréed in a powerful blender.

Cook with chilli seeds: When I'm cooking a dish that requires some spice and heat, such as a bean chilli, stir-fry, ramen (pages 53-5) or huevos rancheros (pages 95-7), I will often include the seeds as well as the flesh of a fresh chilli. Be aware that the seeds are hotter so if you would usually add the flesh of one diced chilli, you might only need to add half, plus the seeds. This varies from chilli to chilli so start with less, taste and add more if needed. The seeds can be added fresh, saved for a few days in a jar and added or dried to fully preserve them.

⚘ Stalks

In most cases, chilli and pepper stalks should be composted. Amazingly though, chilli stalks do contain the good bacteria cultures needed to naturally ferment milk into yogurt. There has been successful research into doing this using cow's milk. However, plant milk is somewhat trickier! If you have a yogurt maker and fancy experimenting, try replacing your starter with ten to 15 chilli stalks, which should be removed once cultured. It's best to choose good quality plant milk with a low percentage of water if you plan to try this.

☑ My favourite ways to compleat:

Dried chilli seeds, flakes and paprika: These can be made in a dehydrator or dried in an oven on the lowest temperature, around 60°C/140°F/gas mark ¼ for four to five hours. Although it does take a long time, these are well worth making if you have grown or want to preserve a large amount of chillies. Use them as you would shop bought chilli flakes but keep in mind that the chillies you use will affect the heat of the flakes. Red chillies are most commonly used. To make, chop the chillies and seeds into small pieces and spread them evenly on a baking tray. Cook until they are fully dried and brittle, checking every hour. Store in a jar and use as is or grind into a powder or smaller flakes using a pestle and mortar or blender. Paprika powder is made by following a similar process using a special variety of peppers. You could try making your own using red bell

peppers or from homegrown peppers selected for this purpose. Follow the same steps to dry your peppers and grind them to a powder using a powerful blender or spice grinder.

Padron peppers: Often served as part of tapas, these are eaten whole (excluding the stalk). Cook the padron peppers over a high heat in a pan with a little olive oil for a few minutes until they soften slightly, and the skin blisters and chars. Serve hot with a generous sprinkling of sea salt. Simple but deliciously sweet and savoury. Perfect with bruschetta and olives or my stuffed cauliflower leaves (pages 73–4).

Chilli oil: Great as a present or for drizzling over dishes, you can infuse olive oil with chilli, garlic or other herbs and spices. See pages 236–7 for my guide.

Homemade harissa sauce: This spicy sauce can be stirred through couscous or pasta, used as a marinade or rub for baked tofu or vegetables, such as aubergine/eggplant or cauliflower, or mixed into hummus or a plant-based yogurt or mayonnaise to add some smoky heat. Slice one medium tomato and two red peppers into chunks. Place in an ovenproof dish with two red chillies. Remove the stalks from the chillies and peppers, but all of the flesh and seeds from both can be added. This sauce is a medium heat but add more chillies if you like it really hot. Also add two peeled garlic cloves and one teaspoon of olive oil. Roast in the oven at 190°C/375°F/gas mark 5 for around 30 minutes until the skins start to char. Remove from the oven and allow to cool. Most recipes say to remove the pepper and chilli skins at this point. I prefer to include the skins because they are full of flavour and blend into the sauce anyway, so save yourself a job! Place the cooled, roasted ingredients in a blender with ¼ teaspoon salt, ½ teaspoon ground cumin and ½ teaspoon smoked paprika and blitz until smooth. Add ¼ teaspoon optional lemon juice, or more, to taste.

My Vegan Huevos Rancheros

Huevos rancheros is a traditional Mexican brunch, and one of my favourite recipes. I love to cook it on Sunday mornings, served with avocado and warm bread. Here, the eggs are replaced with tofu, which is poached in the rich and lightly spiced tomato sauce to absorb the flavours. Although customary as brunch, this dish is hearty enough to be served at any time of the day.

Prep 10 minutes **Cooking** 40 minutes
Serves 4

- 1 teaspoon rapeseed/canola oil
- 1 medium white onion, diced
- 2 garlic cloves, finely diced
- ½ fresh red chilli, diced, plus optional seeds
- 1 red bell pepper, chopped into large chunks
- 1 small courgette/zucchini, diced
- 2 dried bay leaves
- 1½ teaspoons smoked paprika

- 400g/14oz can chopped tomatoes (or make your own, recipe page 222)
- 400g/14oz pack firm unpressed organic tofu
- 60g/2½oz fresh spinach
- Salt and black pepper

To serve:
- 1–2 avocados
- Sourdough or bread of your choice
- Small bunch of fresh coriander/cilantro

1   Heat the rapeseed/canola oil in a sauté pan with a lid. Add the onion and cook over a medium heat for 5 minutes. Stir in the chilli (include the chilli seeds if you wish, depending how hot you like it), garlic, red pepper and courgette.

2   After a few minutes, add the bay leaves and smoked paprika. Mix and let cook for a couple of minutes before adding the chopped tomatoes. Season with a little salt and pepper and cover with the lid. Allow to simmer for 10 minutes.

3   Drain the tofu and chop into 2.5cm/1in cubes. After the 10 minutes, add the cubed tofu to the pan. It should be evenly spaced and sit in the sauce so that it can poach. Return the lid and allow to simmer for around 15 minutes.

You're aiming for the sauce to reduce a little and the tofu to absorb the flavours. Stir from time to time and use your judgement about removing the lid if the sauce needs to reduce a bit more.

4 After the 15 minutes, stir the spinach into the pan and allow it to wilt into the sauce for a few minutes. Meanwhile, remove the flesh from the avocado and warm the bread, ready for serving. Remove the pan from the heat and carefully remove the bay leaves from the sauce.

5 Serve on plates with sliced avocado and warm bread. Chop over fresh coriander leaves and stems.

Green-fingered ideas

The seeds from both chillies and peppers can be planted to grow a new plant with very little effort. Start your seeds in a shallow tray with compost that is 3–5cm/1–2in deep. Keep moist and place in a warm sunny spot, like your windowsill or a greenhouse. Seedlings should appear after one week. Once they are big enough to handle, carefully repot each seedling so that they can develop into individual plants. Plant outside in pots or the ground over summer and keep inside during colder weather to enjoy fresh chillies and peppers grown from leftover seeds.

Citrus fruits

I love lemon drizzle cake, but traditional recipes throw away so much of the fruit. Try my no-waste orange cake recipe (pages 102–3), which uses the entire orange. It can also be swapped with other citrus fruits, for example to create a tangy lemon and lime cake. Citrus fruits also have amazing cleaning properties. The used halves of lemons that often go to waste make ideal scrubbers for your bath or kitchen sink, or infuse vinegar to create a naturally antibacterial spray. And that sad lemon that's sitting untouched in your fridge – slice and freeze it for a refreshing twist to add to drinks.

IN SEASON: January – March

MAKE IT LAST! Citrus fruits last longer when stored in the fridge. If you lack space or want to save them for later, try freezing in slices which you can later add to drinks. Or save the juice in ice cube trays to add to dishes as and when needed.

NUTRITIONAL BENEFITS:
All citrus fruits are an excellent source of vitamin C. The peels are especially rich in antioxidants and actually contain more vitamin C than the flesh. Vitamin C has many important roles, including boosting immunity, helping with iron absorption and creating collagen.

Citrus fruits were named as part of the "dirty dozen" in recent research. This means that unfortunately they are high on the list of produce with multiple pesticide residues, so it's especially worth buying organic if you can and washing the fruit well.

EDIBLE AND USEFUL PARTS:
Flesh, skin, seeds and juice.

• **Tip:** Roll citrus fruits on a hard surface before juicing to make it easier to squeeze and to ensure that you get the maximum juice out of the fruit.

⊡ Peel

The outer peel is edible and adds a zesty tang to cakes, cocktails and salads. Try grating the leftover rinds of squeezed lemons through couscous or grains to add flavour. If you plan to use the zest or peel, choose unwaxed citrus fruits or scrub under a warm tap before use. Some amazing designers have even started making fibre for clothing from this otherwise wasted by-product of orange juice.

Lemon-infused olive oil: Pour 250ml/9fl oz/1 cup of olive oil into a saucepan. Add the peels of three lemons, or more if you need to use them up. Simmer on a low heat for 15 minutes and then strain into a glass bottle.

Orange peel tea: Fresh citrus peels can be steeped in boiling water to create tea. You can also dry the peels by spreading them evenly on a plate and leaving for a few days before storing in a jar to use later. I love Chai tea and you can make a similarly sweet and spicy brew using peelings. In a mug, steep four to five pieces of orange peel in hot water for a few minutes with one mug's worth of black tea (from leaves or a tea bag) to reach the desired strength. Be careful that the black tea does not overpower the citrus flavour. This can be simmered on the hob with a small stick of cinnamon, two cloves and a grating of nutmeg, but for a quick tea simply stir in ½ teaspoon of ground cinnamon and a splash of plant milk.

Save for mulled wine: Dry your orange peelings, as above, and save them in a jar to add to mulled wine.

Citrus leftovers cordial/syrup with bonus candied peels: This cordial uses any leftover citrus peels and spent halves. First, weigh your peels and halves and place them in a jar with the same weight of caster/superfine sugar. Then, muddle well and seal the jar. Leave this overnight and you will wake up to a sweet citrus liquid. If the sugar has not quite dissolved, muddle a little more, add a small splash of water and leave for a few more hours. When ready, carefully remove the peels and halves, making sure to squeeze out all of the liquid. The finished liquid can be used as a cordial to add to water, tonic or cocktails; or as a syrup to drizzle over cakes or pancakes. Store in a jar in the fridge for up to a month. The used peels and halves can then be composted or turned into candied peels. To candy, slice into thin pieces and lay evenly on a baking tray/sheet lined with greaseproof paper. Coat with a light dusting of icing/confectioners' sugar and cook in the oven at the lowest temperature available for roughly 40 minutes, until candied and easy to bite. Store in a jar and eat as is, add to cakes and desserts, or dip in melted dark chocolate and set in the fridge.

Citrus peel-infused gin or vodka: Citrus peels can be used to infuse spirits. See my simple recipe on pages 235–6 and experiment with combinations like lime peel gin and orange peel vodka.

🍵🍸 Flesh and juice

Add the juice to dressings, drinks or cakes and squeeze over pancakes. Try making homemade citrus juice or enjoy slices of orange added to salads.

Homemade lemonade: Peel one lemon, removing as much skin and pith as possible. Save this for blitzing into cakes or freeze the twists of peel to add when serving. Roughly chop the lemon and blend in a food processor with two tablespoons of sugar and 240ml/9fl oz/1 cup of water until liquidized. Dilute to taste with more water; or double the quantities for more lemonade. Strain out the seeds but leave the tasty pulp. Serve over ice with optional peel twists, fresh mint leaves or strawberry leaves.

Plant-based buttermilk: The acidity in lemons is perfect for making a plant-based buttermilk. Mix 1½ tablespoons of fresh lemon juice into 80ml/2½fl oz/1/3 cup of soya milk and two tablespoons of soya yogurt until it curdles. This is useful for baking and batters or as a tangy dressing. See pages 92–3 for my jalapeño poppers recipe using this buttermilk.

☑ My favourite ways to compleat:

Preserved citrus fruits: Scrub and slice whole lemons and layer them in a jar, tightly packed with generous amounts of sea salt between each layer. Add any other herbs and spices (such as a sprig of rosemary, garlic clove, whole chilli or a few peppercorns), squash the lemons down well and top with sea salt. Leave to ferment in the sealed jar for roughly three months, rotating regularly. Once complete, these can be blended into hummus or chopped into a tagine or curry. You can also make preserved limes and oranges with the same method.

Lemon and ginger tea: A great pick-me-up if you're feeling under the weather. Perfect for sore throats and to give your immune system a natural boost. To make your own, squeeze the juice of half a lemon between two mugs then slice the leftovers and add to the mugs. Slice or grate a 2cm/¾in piece of root ginger (you can leave the skin on) and divide between the mugs. Steep with boiling water for a few minutes and enjoy when cool enough. I like to add a few leaves of fresh mint, or you can sweeten it with a little sugar or agave syrup. This is also refreshing served chilled in the summer with mint and ice.

Compleat Recipe: Whole Orange Cake

Sweet, moist and waste-free, this cake is a lovely twist on the more traditional lemon drizzle. You can also follow the same steps with whatever citrus fruits you have at home – perhaps a whole lemon and lime cake or a blend of orange and lemon.

Prep 20 minutes **Cooking** 1 hour

- 135ml/4.5fl oz/½ cup aquafaba (from a can of chickpeas/garbanzo beans. Save the legumes for another dish)
- 250g/9oz/1¼ cups sugar
- 275g/9¾oz/2 cups plain/ all-purpose flour
- 2½ teaspoons baking powder
- 100g/3½oz/scant ½ cup plant butter, plus extra for greasing
- 110g/4oz/scant ½ cup plain plant-based yogurt
- 1 large orange, washed, unpeeled and cut into pieces. Remove any seeds

To serve:
- Citrus syrup and candied peels (recipe on page 100, optional)

1 Preheat the oven to 175°C/350°F/gas mark 4. Lightly grease a 20cm/8in cake tin.

2 In a bowl, whisk the aquafaba until frothy. Add the sugar and whisk until creamy and glossy.

3 Sift in the flour and baking powder then whisk in the butter. Once combined, stir in the yogurt.

4 In a food processor, blend the whole orange pieces until almost puréed. Add this to the cake mixture and stir until combined. Pour into the prepared tin.

5 Bake for 50–60 minutes until the top is golden brown, checking after 50 minutes. To test if your cake is ready, insert a knife into the centre and it is ready if the knife comes out clean.

6 Leave to cool for 15 minutes in the tin before serving. Delicious as is, or drizzle over a little optional citrus syrup and top with candied peels.

Green-fingered ideas

Grow your own plant: Citrus seeds can be planted during spring and summer. This can be a fun experiment, but don't expect success every time! To try, wash the seeds and plant them when fresh roughly 1cm/ ½in deep in a pot with soil. Keep this moist on a warm windowsill, in a greenhouse, or create a cloche with an old clear plastic bottle or tub to form a mini greenhouse until seedlings begin to appear. Although the plants may not fruit, they are lovely as a house plant and orange and lemon leaves can be steeped in boiling water to make a refreshing tea.

Natural gardening uses: Orange peels are beneficial for soil as a natural fertilizer. Tear them up and bury in your garden. They will release nutrients and nitrogen into the soil as they decompose.

Citrus peels scattered in your flower beds are also thought to deter cats from using your garden as a toilet. It is believed that our feline friends dislike the citrusy scent.

♻ Household projects and ideas

Cut down on plastic in your home by making your own cleaning products. Lemon and lime both have antibacterial properties and are brilliant natural cleaners (method follows).

Grapefruit peels cleaning scrub: Grapefruit peels are useful in the home. First, dry the peels out on a plate for a few days until brittle. Next, blend these in a food processor to a powder. Mix one part dried ground peels with one part coarse salt and one part bicarbonate of soda/baking soda. This makes a great cleaning scrub for your bathroom, sinks and tiles.

Waste-Free, Toxin-Free Lemon Cleaner Two Ways

Lemon is naturally antibacterial and perfect for creating a multipurpose cleaning spray. The essential oils in its skin have disinfectant properties, and the scent is much more pleasant than chemical cleaners. This spray is toxin-free and waste-free – making it better for you, your home and our waterways. Pair this spray with plastic-free cleaning materials. I use a compostable coconut scrubber and washable bamboo kitchen towel.

For the spray:
- Distilled white vinegar
- 1 lemon (or lime)
- Any leftover citrus skins or juice
- Fresh rosemary, mint or lavender (optional)

For the scrub:
- Leftover lemon or lime halves
- Bicarbonate of soda/baking soda

You will also need:
- An old spray bottle (or make one by reusing a bottle and purchasing a spray top)

1 Mix one part white vinegar with one part water and fill your container three-quarters of the way up.

2 Using a fine mesh sieve/strainer over a bowl, squeeze the juice from your citrus fruit. Be careful not to let any of the pulp or seeds through as this will block your spray pump. Then use a funnel to pour the juice into your container.

3 Add any leftover fresh citrus juice you may have from cooking or other projects and seal the top. Your cleaning spray is ready to go!

4 To really get the benefits of the essential oils, carefully peel a few strips of skin from your lemon or lime and add these to the container. This isn't essential but the peelings will gradually infuse your spray and help boost its cleaning properties. You could also add offcuts of fresh herbs, such as rosemary, mint or lavender.

5 You'll now be left with the halves of your lemon or lime. These can be composted or saved in an airtight container in the fridge for up to 3 days until you want to use them.

6 When ready, microwave the citrus halves for 15 seconds. This helps to wake them up and leaves your microwave smelling fresh. Carefully, remove them from the microwave. Use them to scrub the bath, skins, taps and areas with a build-up of limescale or soap scum.

7 This naturally cuts through grease and dirt, but to make your job even easier, scatter a little bicarbonate of soda/baking soda on the area and rub with the citrus halves. This combination is naturally fungicidal and abrasive.

Coconut

We don't often buy a fresh coconut, but we do frequently use its by-products – such as coconut milk, oil, sugar and water. Making these yourself can be fun and really intensifies the coconut flavour. In India, the coconut tree is known as the tree which provides everything needed for life. This is because every part has a use – the fruit is edible, and other parts like the coir, shell and leaves can be used for clothing, homewares, containers and, as a tree, for shade.

IN SEASON: Coconuts are available year-round but are grown in tropical climates, so it's worth considering the carbon footprint of this.

MAKE IT LAST! Fresh whole coconuts should be stored at room temperature. Once cracked, store in a container in the fridge and use as soon as possible.

NUTRITIONAL BENEFITS: Coconut flesh is really nutritious and full of fibre, vitamins B1, B3, B5, B6, C and E, and minerals like iron, calcium and magnesium. This is more so when fresh than canned or packaged. Coconut water can be hydrating and contains some sugars and potassium.

EDIBLE AND USEFUL PARTS: Flesh, liquid and shell.

☐ How to prepare a coconut

If you haven't prepared a whole coconut before then it can be a little intimidating. First, remove any of the outer hairy fibres. These are often sparse by the time coconuts arrive in our shops but if you have lots then compost those, use them as twine or try weaving them to make a natural dish scrubber. Then place the whole coconut in the oven at 180°C/350°F/gas mark 4 for 20 minutes. Allow to cool at room temperature before poking a skewer through the softest of the small round holes to drain and collect the water. Wrap the coconut in a dish towel and carefully tap it with a hammer near the hole to break the shell and reveal the tasty flesh. If you plan to make something from the shell, then you might prefer to crack it open using a saw to make a straight cut. Job done!

☺ Flesh

The white coconut flesh is delicious raw. You can also use a peeler to create coconut shavings, which can be scattered over dishes like dahl (page 146).

Coconut milk: The white flesh of a fresh coconut can quickly be made into coconut milk. In a blender, process the chopped coconut flesh (around 100g/3½oz) with a pinch of sea salt and 500ml/17fl oz/2 cups water – if you have the water from your fresh coconut then include that in this. Blend for around one minute until liquidized. You could strain out the pulp but there is really no need as this adds taste! Add more or less water to achieve your desired consistency, whether using the milk as a drink or for cooking into curry, dahl (page 146) or soup (pages 206-7). This makes roughly 500ml/ 17fl oz/2 cups, or just over the equivalent of one shop-bought can of coconut milk. Store in a jar in the fridge for a few days or freeze in a tub.

Toasted coconut chips: I love these as a snack; they are great on the go, as well as added to cakes, granola (pages 238-9) or cookies. Using a peeler, peel even strips from the white coconut flesh, including the flesh's thin brown skin – a bit like crisps. Spread these evenly on a baking tray and cook in the oven at 160°C/315°F/gas mark 2-3 for five to ten minutes. Mix halfway through cooking and check frequently – it should smell amazing. The finished chips should be browned but not burned. You can season these with a little salt, spices or sweetener, but I prefer the natural coconut taste. Store in an airtight jar and eat within two weeks.

Desiccated coconut: This is useful for baking, as well as other recipes, and can quickly be made from the whit flesh of a fresh coconut. First, chop or peel the flesh into small pieces. Then, add this to a blender and blitz with no liquid so that you create fine coconut gratings. This will naturally be a bit moist, so place it in a frying pan over a low heat and stir frequently for five to ten minutes until the coconut is dry and ready to use. Add to dishes like energy balls, coconut cake, flapjacks, tiffin or curries.

🥛 Liquid

The liquid from a fresh coconut is known as coconut water and can be enjoyed as a drink or added to cocktails, ice lollies, sorbet and smoothies. You can also use this instead of water when cooking rice to infuse the grain with extra flavour.

🥥 Shells

Coconut shells and fibres are used to produce lots of products, such as homewares like bowls, brushes, scrubbers, ropes and door mats. The coir is also often added to garden compost. Not only are these made from a by-product, but they are also usually compostable at the end of their life cycles.

Homemade bird feeder: It can be so rewarding to feed birds in your garden or balcony. A simple feeder can be made by drilling small holes through a halved coconut shell, tying with twine and stuffing the shell with your choice of bird feed.

Coconut bowl: If you are careful when cutting your coconut, the shell halves could be used to make a beautiful bowl. To achieve a smooth finish, sand the shells well. This is easier with tools but can be done by hand with sandpaper and determination! Once sanded, coat the inside and outside of the bowl with five layers of vegetable oil, allowing it to dry briefly and absorb the oil between each layer. Your bowl is then complete. The oil can be reapplied every year or so as and when needed.

Coconut shell planter: To create a planter from your halved coconut shells, follow the same steps as when making a bowl. Sand and oil as much as you wish, but you could leave the surface rough and textured. These are great for using in a small macramé plant hanger, or you could make your own simple coconut shell plant hanger. Carefully drill three equally spaced holes at the top of the shell half, thread twine through each hole and secure at a point at the top.

Corn

Delicious cooked whole over a barbeque, there are many ways to make use of every part of an ear of corn. The husks are durable and therefore commonly used to make Mexican tamales. The cob and other parts we usually throw away are actually full of flavour and perfect for making a sweet broth. We often don't, but a sweetcorn ear is so worth buying whole and complete.

IN SEASON: August - October.

MAKE IT LAST! Fresh corn is best stored in the fridge. You could also freeze cobs with the kernels attached, ready to boil and eat later; or remove the kernels using a knife and freeze or refrigerate those.

NUTRITIONAL BENEFITS: Sweetcorn is high in vitamin C and a good source of fibre and thiamine. The cob, husks and silks are also nutritious and full of flavour. Sweetcorn was named as part of the "clean 15" in recent research. This means that it was found to contain little, if any, pesticide residues!

EDIBLE AND USEFUL PARTS: Kernels, cobs, husks and silks.

⊡ Kernels

Fresh corn kernels taste amazingly sweet and have a satisfying bite compared with a can of sweetcorn. Enjoy them as a classic corn on the cob, boiled or charred on the barbeque. To remove the kernels from the cob, stand the uncooked cob upright in a sturdy bowl and run a knife down the length of the corn. Add these to salads, bean burgers, relish and more.

Fresh sweetcorn relish: Light and full of flavour, this salsa-style relish is made with fresh kernels and is great served with salad, tortillas or a jacket potato. To make it, remove the kernels from one sweetcorn cob (the equivalent of roughly 115g/4oz). Add these to a frying pan with one teaspoon of dried chilli flakes and a little salt and pepper. Toast over a medium heat for five minutes, stirring frequently. It will begin to crackle, and the kernels should turn a bright yellow colour, with slight charring. Add to a bowl with around ten diced cherry tomatoes, one diced shallot (or ¼ diced red onion), the juice of half a lime and a handful of chopped fresh coriander/cilantro leaves and stalks. Try this served with my stuffed corn husk parcels, recipe follows on pages 112–13.

Roasted sweetcorn kernels: Great as a snack on the go, these can be seasoned with your choice of flavourings, such as smoked paprika, chilli powder or garlic powder. Toss the kernels in a little oil and season with salt, pepper and any other seasonings, so that they are well coated. Bake evenly on a tray at 180°C/350°F/gas mark 4 for 15–20 minutes until crispy.

▦ Cobs, husks and silks

When you buy a fresh ear of sweetcorn, the cob, husks and silks (those stringy tufts) are usually discarded. Although not edible, these are useful. The husks are strong and used for making tamales, as well as to create things like paper and woven homewares.

Stuffed corn husk parcels

As with a banana leaf, corn husks can be used to seal and bake or barbeque food, imparting a subtle flavour. I like to stuff them with a simple homemade vegan cheeze, which should be prepared a few days in advance.

Prep 30 minutes, (plus two days in advance for the cheese)
Cooking 15 minutes **Serves** 4

For the cheeze:
- 120g/4¼oz raw cashews
- 3 tablespoons melted refined/ flavourless coconut oil
- 2 teaspoons lemon juice
- 1 teaspoon salt
- 1/8 teaspoon garlic powder

For the parcels:
- 1 husk of one ear of corn per person
- 1 garlic clove per parcel

1   To make the cheeze, soak the cashews in a bowl of water overnight. The following day, strain and add the cashews to a blender with the coconut oil, lemon juice, salt and garlic powder. Blend until smooth and decant into a tub to refrigerate overnight. In the morning the cheeze will be firmer and ready to eat.

2   Time to make the corn husk parcels! When removing the corn from inside the husks, try to keep the husks in a secure bowl-like shape. Save the corn kernels to make a relish or barbeque them on the cob. If your husks have kept their shape then great, just check that they are secure enough to hold the cheeze. Otherwise, carefully lay the husk leaves horizontally across a plate to create a husk parcel.

3   When ready, place two chunks of cheeze in the centre of each husk, along with a garlic clove. You can leave the skin on the clove for cooking but smash it slightly with the side of a knife to wake it up. Layer the remaining husks over each one to seal them into little parcels. Pinch the end of each and use a thin strip of husk to tie it closed.

4 These can be cooked directly on a barbeque for five to ten minutes to achieve a smoky charring or placed on a baking tray and cooked in the oven at 190°C/375°F/gas mark 5 for 15 minutes.

5 Serve with sweetcorn relish (recipe on page 111), salad or corn on the cob. Eat this directly from the husks, which can be composted after use.

Sweetcorn silk tea: This tea is popular for its health benefits. The silks have been found to be anti-inflammatory and a natural source of antioxidants. Silk herbal tea is sold in health food shops, so why not try making your own. To do so, steep a small amount of the silks in boiled water for a few minutes before straining and drinking. You can add things like fresh mint or agave syrup to balance out the sweetcorn-like taste. The silks can also be dried out at room temperature for a few days and saved in a jar for a few months to have a ready supply of tea.

Sweetcorn broth: This sweet but savoury broth is great for using as a base for soups like ramen and chowder or adding to dishes like risotto and stews. To make, place the cobs, husks and silks from at least two ears of sweetcorn in a large saucepan and fill with water. Cover with a lid and bring to the boil and simmer for roughly 45 minutes. It should release a lovely sweet aroma and taste sweet but earthy. Strain out the cobs, husks and silks and compost those. Once cooled, decant the broth into containers and store in the fridge for up to a week or freeze.

Compleat Recipe: Mexican-Spiced Sweetcorn Chowder

This chowder gets its subtly sweet flavour from a homemade broth of sweetcorn cobs, husks and silks. This can be made in advance and stored in the fridge for up to a week. If you are making the broth on the same day, remove the kernels from the sweetcorn ear using a knife and set aside whilst the broth simmers for 45 minutes (recipe on page 113). Fresh kernels are best but if you don't have those then a small can or frozen sweetcorn kernels can be used as an alternative.

Prep 10 minutes **Cooking** 20 minutes, plus 45 minutes for the broth
Serves 4

- 2 teaspoons rapeseed/canola oil
- 1 red onion, diced
- 2 garlic cloves, finely chopped
- 1 medium carrot, chopped
- 1 red, orange or yellow pepper, chopped
- ¼ teaspoon medium chilli powder
- ½ teaspoon smoked paprika
- ¼ teaspoon ground cumin
- ½ teaspoon dried mixed herbs
- Kernels from 2 ears of corn (200g/7oz fresh or 220g/8oz frozen)
- 800ml/28fl oz/scant 3½ cups homemade sweetcorn broth
- 1 teaspoon tomato purée/paste
- Salt

To serve:
- Handful of chopped fresh coriander/cilantro
- Lime juice
- Homemade tortilla chips

1   Heat the oil in a large saucepan over a medium heat and add the red onion. After a couple of minutes add the garlic cloves, carrot and pepper. Stir and allow to cook for a few minutes before adding the chilli powder, smoked paprika, cumin and mixed herbs. Mix well and add the sweetcorn kernels.

2   Pour in the sweetcorn broth and bring to a simmer. Add the tomato purée and allow to simmer for 10 minutes with the lid on. Remove from the heat and, using a hand blender, roughly blend for 30 seconds so that some of the kernels are puréed but the broth retains a nice texture. Taste and season with a little salt.

3   Serve hot with chopped fresh coriander, a squeeze of lime per bowl and an optional handful of freshly baked tortilla chips.

Courgette/zucchini

There are so many ways to prepare this delicious summer squash. I especially love courgettes raw in salads, added in ribbons to a stir-fry or baked in a herby tomato sauce. At our allotment, we've sworn not to grow courgettes again because they produce such a huge harvest that we could live all year just on the ones other people give away! If you're in the same boat, try freezing or pickling your courgettes to enjoy a supply over winter, or roast them in batches of pasta sauce and freeze ready to defrost and cook.

IN SEASON: June – September

MAKE IT LAST! Courgettes are best stored in the fridge. If you have an abundance of courgettes you'd like to freeze, I recommend grating them into portions before freezing. After defrosting, squeeze out the flesh to remove any excess moisture. Grated courgette is great for adding to savoury pancake mixes, fritters and pasta sauces.

NUTRITIONAL BENEFITS: Courgettes are a good source of vitamin C, potassium and fibre. The skin is particularly rich in fibre, whilst the flesh is packed with water and very few calories – to which it owes its popularity as a light food choice.

EDIBLE AND USEFUL PARTS: Flesh, skin, seeds and flowers.

▣ ▣ Flesh and skin

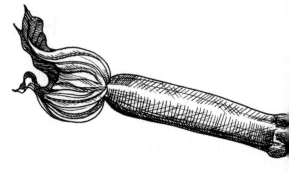

When preparing a courgette, I remove just a small part of the stalk end, as this tends to be too hard to eat. This end can be added to a veggie offcuts broth (recipe on pages 232–4). The flesh, skin and even flowers are otherwise edible. The taste is quite different when raw and I especially like to add raw slices and ribbons to salads or wraps with other vegetables. Switch up a stir-fry by incorporating ribbons of courgette and carrot, or chop courgette into stews and pasta sauces or as a topping for pizza.

▣ Flowers

Depending on local availability, or if you grow your own, you may be able to source some courgette flowers. These can be stuffed with cashew cream cheeze, fried in batter or baked into dishes.

Courgette flower egg-free "omelette": This "omelette", topped with courgette flowers, makes enough for a small frying pan, with a lid – perfect for two to share. Double the quantities for a large pan for four. Carefully remove the stamen from four courgette flowers and tear each flower into two to three strips and set aside. In a bowl, mix 60g/2½oz/scant ½ cup chickpea/gram/garbanzo flour with two tablespoons nutritional yeast. Mix well with a hand whisk before adding 100ml/3½fl oz/scant ½ cup water. Season and mix well with a fork or hand whisk to remove any clumps until smooth. Set aside. Chop one third of a small courgette, one quarter of a small onion and one garlic clove, and sauté in a frying pan with a little plant butter for five to seven minutes until starting to colour. Pour over the wet mix and scatter the flowers evenly on the top. Sprinkle one teaspoon nutritional yeast over the top. Cook with the lid on over a medium heat for around five minutes until golden on the outside and softer inside.

☑ My favourite ways to compleat:

Pickled: Courgettes and red onions work well pickled together in slices with some mustard seeds, peppercorns and a bay leaf. Turn to page 235 for my easy pickling recipe. Great for preserving a big harvest of courgettes.

Vegetable kebabs: Chop courgettes into chunks with other vegetables, like aubergine/eggplant, cherry tomatoes, mushrooms, red onion and pepper, and cook on skewers over a barbeque or under the grill/broiler until slightly charred and hot.

Ratatouille: Chop one large aubergine/eggplant, one to two courgettes and one red pepper into cubes, and slice five cloves of garlic. In a saucepan, heat three tablespoons olive oil and add the aubergine first, with one tablespoon salt. Cook on a medium heat for five minutes before adding the courgettes, pepper and garlic. Cook for a further seven to ten minutes then add four large chopped fresh tomatoes or a tin of plum tomatoes. Simmer for 20 minutes, encouraging the tomatoes to break down after around ten minutes. Once cooked, stir through a handful of chopped fresh herbs, like oregano and basil. Delicious served as is or with my onion-skin infused focaccia, recipe on page 170-1.

Tomato baked courgettes: This dish is a great way to use up an abundance of courgettes. Thinly slice as many courgettes as you wish - using a variety of green, yellow and white courgettes can be nice. Layer them in a dish with a herby tomato sauce, such as my homemade roasted tomato sauce recipe on page 222, and bake in the oven at 180°C/350°F/gas mark 4 for around 30 minutes.

Compleat Recipe: Courgette and Banana Peel Loaf Cake

This loaf cake is lightly spiced and provides some added goodness by including courgette and otherwise-wasted banana skins. Brown banana skins are best, and I collect mine in an airtight container in the fridge until I have enough to use in dishes. They keep well for a few days – use your judgement. If you don't have peels to hand, replace these with the flesh of one banana, mashed and added.

Prep 20 minutes **Cooking** 1 hour
Makes 1 loaf cake

- 100g/3½oz banana skins (saved from 2-3 bananas. No need to remove the white stringy bits called the phloem bundles.)
- 250g/9oz/1¾ cups plain/all-purpose flour
- 150g/5oz/¾ cup caster/superfine sugar
- 1 tablespoon baking powder
- 1 teaspoon ground cinnamon
- 1 teaspoon ground ginger
- ¼ teaspoon ground nutmeg
- ¼ teaspoon salt
- 140g/5oz courgettes/zucchini
- 75ml/2½fl oz/1/3 cup vegetable oil
- 60ml/2fl oz/¼ cup plant milk

1   Wash the banana skins, remove the hard ends and chop the rest into small pieces. Add to a saucepan of water, bring to the boil and simmer for 10 minutes. Strain, saving 60ml/2fl oz/¼ cup of the water in a bowl along with the boiled skins. Purée the mix in a blender until smooth. Set aside.

2   Preheat the oven to 180°C/350°F/gas mark 4 and line a 23 x 13cm/9 x 5in loaf tin with non-stick baking paper.

3   In a bowl, combine the dry ingredients. Grate in the courgette and add the puréed banana peel, oil and plant milk. Mix well. It may seem dry at first but the courgette will release moisture once stirred.

4   Pour the cake mix into the prepared tin. Bake in the middle of the oven for 30 minutes, then cover with aluminium foil and bake for a further 20 minutes.

Remove from the oven and after five minutes, remove from the tin and serve warm or allow to cool on a wire/cooling rack.

⊞ Green-fingered ideas

If you grow courgettes, then you'll know they can quickly turn overly large and marrow-like before your eyes! However, these are still tasty and are especially great for adding a creamy taste to vegetable soup. Try cooking your chopped courgettes/marrow with some onion and garlic before adding stock, canned chopped tomatoes, curry powder, ground cumin, chilli powder and seasoning to taste. Once softened, blend using a hand blender. This can be frozen in portions in airtight containers once cooled to give you a supply of warming soup over the colder months. Interestingly, the leaves from young courgette plants are also edible and can be used as you would other greens.

Cucumber

Cucumbers are useful for more than just salad. Try slices in summer rolls, pickled or added to drinks. When preparing a cucumber, eat right down to the very end, excluding just the stalk, and there's no need to remove the peel. You could even use any cucumber offcuts to infuse or add to spirits and cocktails, such as gin (see how on pages 235–6).

IN SEASON: May – August

MAKE IT LAST! Cucumbers are best stored in the fridge. If you'd like to preserve a glut of cucumbers, try pickling them.

NUTRITIONAL BENEFITS: Cucumbers are rich in vitamin K, and there's no need to remove the peel, it's full of fibre.

EDIBLE AND USEFUL PARTS: Flesh, skin and seeds.

☑ My favourite ways to compleat:

Summer rolls: These raw vegetable-filled rice rolls look impressive but are very easy to make. Slice vegetables such as radish, cucumber, carrot, spring onion/scallion and some broccoli stalk into strips. Wrap them in rehydrated rice paper sheets to create little parcels. I love to serve these as a healthy but really satisfying shared main. They work well with sweet chilli or peanut sauce for dipping.

Tzatziki: This is a delicious dip made using cucumber. Grate one whole, unpeeled cucumber into a bowl and combine with 350g/12oz/1½ cups plain plant-based yogurt, the juice of half a lemon, two minced garlic cloves and one teaspoon of olive oil. Delicious and great for dipping falafels and pitta breads.

Pickled cucumber: Slices of cucumber are great pickled and work well with some mustard seeds, fresh chilli and slices of onion. Turn to page 235 for my easy pickling recipe.

Green-fingered ideas

Homegrown cucumbers are beautiful – often much larger and tastier than those from shops. And because they are larger, the seeds from the centre of your cucumber can be saved to plant next year. Rinse your seeds and dry them out fully before storing them in an envelope to sow in spring.

Fennel

Fennel is a flowering plant. Used in sweet and savoury cooking, it has a delicate liquorice-like taste. The whole fennel plant is edible and full of its distinctive flavour. As well as the bulb, the leafy fronds, core and stalks can also be enjoyed. The seeds are also edible and commonly sold for cooking.

IN SEASON: June – September

MAKE IT LAST! Fennel is best stored in the fridge. Pickling is a good way to preserve slices of fennel; try it pickled with aromatics like fennel seeds, peppercorns and mustard seeds.

NUTRITIONAL BENEFITS: Fennel is a good source of potassium, which is important for muscle health, as well as containing a good amount of folate.

EDIBLE AND USEFUL PARTS: Bulb, core, stalks and fronds.

Bulb and core

When raw, the fennel bulb has a strong liquorice-like taste. Try it shredded through salads and slaws. For a deeper but more mellow taste, enjoy the bulb roasted, griddled or charred in wedges on the barbeque. There's no need to remove the "core" – it isn't tough and helps hold the bulb together, especially when the fennel is sliced into wedges.

Roasted fennel: Divide the fennel into wedges and coat in olive oil and balsamic vinegar (around one tablespoon olive oil and one teaspoon balsamic vinegar per bulb). Place in an ovenproof dish and roast at 190°C/375°F/gas mark 5 for 30–40 minutes.

⬘ Stalks

The tall stalks shooting out of the top of the fennel bulb, topped with the fronds are also edible. Shred them finely and there's no need to discard them. They can be cooked like the bulb or chopped through a salad. Fennel stalks are sometimes compared to celery and can be used in a similar way. Try slicing them through a stew, such as my Mediterranean celery stew on pages 81–2, to impart a subtle fennel flavour.

⬙ Fronds:

The fronds are the feathery leaves from the top of the fennel bulb and are full of flavour. Enjoy them cooked or raw. Chop them over a salad or as an addition to a slaw, as well as using them as you would fresh herbs to garnish and season dishes.

Lemony fennel frond olive oil: Finely shred the fronds from one fennel bulb and place in a small bowl with a few tablespoons of olive oil, a squeeze of lemon juice and some salt and pepper. Taste and add more lemon juice or olive oil if needed, depending on your quantity of fronds. Try this drizzled over salad, steamed new potatoes or roasted vegetables.

Fennel infused spirits: With their liquorice-like taste, fennel fronds – and in fact the whole bulb – can infuse spirits. See my simple infusion recipe on pages 235–6 and experiment with combinations, such as fennel vodka or gin.

Fennel frond tea: Many herbal teas use liquorice root to add some sweetness to the brew. Fennel fronds are a tasty alternative. Steep a handful in boiled water and leave for a few minutes before straining and enjoying once cooled a little. Also try a blend of fennel fronds and mint leaves for a refreshing but sweet brew. Fennel tea has also been suggested to aid digestion.

Fennel frond pesto: Fennel fronds can be used to make a homemade pesto. Chop a few into your pesto alongside spinach and other greens. Or for a more potent fennel taste, use just the fronds. Find my pesto recipe on page 158 and taste as you go to achieve your desired flavour.

Add to pickled produce: Add a few fennel fronds to whatever you might be pickling to infuse it with a subtle fennel taste. Try adding these to pickled onions or beetroots.

☑ My favourite ways to compleat:

Root vegetable and fennel gratin: Slice a whole fennel bulb through a creamy baked vegetable gratin and sprinkle through the chopped fronds. Fennel is sweeter and more earthy when baked so it works well with the creamy stock. For my gratin recipe, see pages 77-8, and try a combination of potato and fennel.

Compleat Recipe: Seared Fennel Salad

This salad incorporates the whole fennel bulb and fronds. Cooked over a griddle pan, the fennel has a more delicate taste that really complements the beetroot, olives and cheeze. If you can't find fennel with the fronds, it's not a problem to leave those out, although they do give the plate an extra hint of flavour. This is topped with dollops of a simple, homemade plant-based cheeze which should be prepared a few days in advance. Alternatively, use a shop-bought vegan cream cheeze or ricotta.

Prep 15 minutes, plus making the cheeze **Cooking** 10 minutes
Serves 4 as a starter or 2 as a main

- 1 fennel bulb with fronds
- 2 teaspoons olive oil
- 100g/3½oz fresh spinach
- ½ cucumber, sliced
- 2 beetroots (steamed or pickled), chopped
- 10 pitted green olives

- 1 teaspoon lemon juice
- Salt and black pepper

For the cheeze:
- 120g/4oz raw cashews, soaked
- 3 tablespoons refined/flavourless coconut oil, melted
- 2 teaspoons lemon juice
- 1 teaspoon salt
- 1/8 teaspoon garlic powder

1 To make the cheeze, soak the cashews in water overnight. The next day, strain and add the cashews to a blender with the melted coconut oil, lemon juice, salt and garlic powder. Blend until smooth and decant into a tub to refrigerate overnight. In the morning the cheeze will be firm and ready to eat.
2 To make the salad, remove the fronds from the fennel and set aside. Slice the rest of the whole bulb, plus any stalks, lengthways into 5mm/¼in wide wedges. In a bowl, toss the sliced fennel in the olive oil so that it is well coated. Add a little salt and pepper to season to taste.
3 Heat a griddle pan over a medium to high heat. Place the fennel wedges in the pan and cook for 5 minutes on each side until soft and lightly charred.
4 Serve the cooked fennel on a bed of spinach, cucumber, beetroot and olives. Dollop over generous servings of the cheeze and squeeze over the fresh lemon juice. Finely shred the fronds. Scatter these over the top of the plates.

Garlic

Where would our kitchens be without garlic? It's the key to flavour throughout so many cuisines. The cloves are delicious roasted, sautéed, pickled and minced into soups, stews, curries and sauces. The papery skins are also edible and impart rich flavours to broths.

IN SEASON: Available year-round but at its best from July to October.

MAKE IT LAST! Garlic is best stored in a cool, dark place. It can also be minced and frozen ready to cook with, or you could pickle the cloves. If you grow your own garlic then this can be bundled up and dried, as you would fresh herbs. It should be fully dried after a few weeks and can be stored in a mesh bag or woven basket in a cool, dark place with good air circulation.

NUTRITIONAL BENEFITS: Throughout history garlic has been praised for its health benefits, believed to be antioxidant, anti-inflammatory, antibacterial and immunity-boosting, in particular when eaten raw, pickled or fermented. Garlic is high in vitamins B6 and C, manganese and selenium. It is also a good source of phosphorous, calcium, potassium, iron and copper.

EDIBLE AND USEFUL PARTS: Cloves, bulbs and skin.

⬚ Cloves

Add garlic to almost any dish to enhance its flavour: sauté with greens like beet or turnip tops, roast with tomatoes for a homemade chopped tomato sauce, mix into salsas or blend into hummus and pesto. To remove a garlic clove from its skin with minimal waste, slice off a tiny piece of the hard end and then smash the clove with the side of your knife to release the skin. The clove should then pop out – no need to trim off anything else.

Garlic bread: A quick homemade garlic bread is so easy to make and much tastier than those from a shop. Toast a few slices of your bread of choice; ciabatta works well but a regular wholemeal loaf is also surprisingly good. Rub each slice of toasted bread with a peeled garlic clove so that the clove breaks down and flavours the bread. Serve as is or brush with a little olive oil and chopped fresh herbs, such as basil or oregano. Top with chopped fresh tomatoes and red onion to transform this into a bruschetta.

Garlic-infused olive oil: Make your own flavoured oil with a few cloves of garlic and optional herbs. Turn to pages 236-7 for the recipe. Infused oils are delicious as a dressing for salads, pastas and other dishes, or for dipping freshly baked breads.

Frozen garlic butter cubes: Mince a few cloves of fresh garlic and chop some optional fresh herbs, such as basil or oregano. Divide evenly into ice cube trays and fill with olive oil. Freeze and add to dishes as and when needed for a ready-made hit of creamy garlic and herbs.

Roasted garlic cloves: I love to roast individual garlic cloves, by themselves or with vegetables like beetroot, carrots or parsnips. It's so easy to do and achieves an amazingly rich and moreish taste. Separate your garlic cloves but leave the skin on. This protective layer helps seal in the goodness whilst cooking. Place in an ovenproof dish and drizzle with a little olive or rapeseed/canola oil. Bake in the oven at 190°C/375°F/gas mark 5 for 20–25 minutes until the bulbs are soft and caramelized, and the skins a little darkened. Check regularly because garlic can quickly turn from delicious to burned. To serve, pop the gooey contents out of the skins (compost those) and enjoy the garlic whole, tossed through pasta, blended into hummus or smeared over toast.

Pickled garlic cloves: Garlic cloves can be pickled whole or added to other pickled vegetables, such as onions or radishes. Crunchy and full of flavour. See page 235 for my easy pickling recipe.

Sprouted bulbs or cloves

If your garlic sprouts a green shoot, the good news is that it is still edible. This usually happens if your garlic is old or hasn't been stored in a cool or dry enough place. However, you can eat the bulb as usual, as well as any green shoots. The shoots can be chopped and cooked into dishes with the rest of your garlic. These are also perfect for planting to grow more garlic – see my "green-fingered ideas" on page 130.

Skin

Although not commonly eaten, the papery garlic skins are edible and contain goodness and antioxidants. The skins can be boiled into broths or ground and added to dishes.

Garlic skins powder: Add one teaspoon of ground garlic skin to bread dough, such as my focaccia recipe on pages 170-1. The skins can be ground in a mortar and pestle, but for larger amounts use a blender. Whilst the taste is very subtle, it gives an antioxidant boost to your baking. Or try adding this to batter for dishes like battered onion rings, fried tofu or savoury pancakes.

Ramp-up your rice: To give rice an added nutritional boost, steep your garlic skins in the water whilst the rice cooks and remove before serving.

Veggie offcuts broth: Add the skins to a veggie offcuts broth (see pages 232-4). This is how I most commonly use up garlic skins. It produces a deep and flavourful broth which is perfect for soups, stews and more. The skins can be frozen until you have enough to use.

☑ My favourite ways to compleat:

Garlic-skin infused focaccia: In the onion chapter of this book (pages 170-1.) I have included my recipe for a focaccia bread, baked with blended onion skins and topped with caramelized red onions. The onion skin and flesh in this recipe can be replaced with garlic, or you could use a mix of onion and garlic skins and top the bread with caramelized red onion and garlic. Delicious and waste-free.

Fresh pesto or pasta sauce: Garlic cloves can be added raw and unpeeled to sauces, such as pesto, if you are going to blend the sauce anyway – it saves time and waste. My carrot top pesto on page 67 and "salad bag" pesto on page 158 both use one whole, unpeeled garlic clove, as does my cauliflower alfredo pasta sauce on page 71.

Compleat Recipe: Roasted Aubergine and Garlic Baba Ganoush Dip

This Middle Eastern dip is delicious as part of a mezze or just with pitta breads and/or falafels. It is traditionally made by cooking the aubergines/eggplants until charred and blistered. However, the aubergine and garlic skins are usually discarded. My take on this dip uses the whole roasted aubergine fruits, as well as garlic cloves and skins. Not only does this save you a job, but it adds flavour and goodness.

Prep 10 minutes **Cooking** 35 minutes
Makes one generous bowl

- 2 aubergines/eggplants
- 4 garlic cloves, unpeeled
- 3 teaspoons olive oil

- Any leftover garlic skins you want to use up (optional)
- 1 tablespoon lemon juice
- 2 teaspoons tahini
- ½ teaspoon salt
- ½ teaspoon ground cumin

1 Remove the stalk from the aubergines (compost that) and slice the aubergines into quarters. Place these flesh-down in an ovenproof dish with the unpeeled garlic cloves. Drizzle over two teaspoons of the olive oil. Roast at 190°C/375°F/gas mark 5 for 30–35 minutes, until softened. Set aside to cool.

2 Once cooled, place the aubergine and garlic, plus any extra skins you would like to add, in a food processor. Add the remaining olive oil and all of the lemon juice, tahini, salt and cumin. Blend for a few minutes until everything is combined and puréed to your desired consistency.

3 Store in an airtight jar in the fridge and eat within a few days.

⊞ Green-fingered ideas

If your garlic has begun to sprout shoots and you don't want to cook with it, you could plant the cloves. This is best done in autumn or early winter because garlic likes cold in order to develop, but you can also try in spring. First, separate the cloves from the bulb. The bigger the clove, the better your crop will be. Garlic can be grown in the ground or in containers. Next, plant the cloves in the same way as daffodil bulbs, burying them with the pointy shoot end up at a depth about twice as long as the clove. Keep moist but be careful not to over water or your bulbs could turn mouldy. Your garlic will be ready to harvest in summer.

Ginger (root)

For years I peeled root ginger before using it, but one day I wondered why. When fresh, the skin is so delicate and soft that there's really no need at all to remove it. For every recipe in this book, the ginger is sliced or grated without peeling. So, save yourself a job, reduce your kitchen waste and add some extra flavour and goodness by compleating your root ginger. Its sweet but fiery taste is perfect in so many dishes, such as my spiced butternut squash soup (pages 206–8), pumpkin curry (pages 191–2), coconutty kale and chickpea dahl (page 146) or a warming ramen (pages 53–5).

IN SEASON: Root ginger is available year-round and is usually grown in Asia.

MAKE IT LAST! Root ginger is best stored at room temperature but should be kept in the fridge once sliced. You could also grate and freeze ginger, ready to add to dishes.

NUTRITIONAL BENEFITS: Ginger has traditionally been used to calm an upset stomach, and is believed to be anti-inflammatory, antibacterial and to help boost immunity – especially helpful if you have a cold. Ginger is rich in potassium but remember that we only tend to eat a small amount of ginger compared with other potassium-rich foods, like bananas.

EDIBLE AND USEFUL PARTS:
Flesh and skin.

☑ My favourite ways to compleat:

Lemon and ginger tea: A great pick-me-up if you're feeling under the weather. Perfect for sore throats and to give your immune system a natural boost. To make your own, squeeze the juice of half a lemon between two mugs then slice the leftovers and add to the mugs. Slice or grate a 2cm/¾in piece of root ginger (you can leave the skin on) and divide between the mugs. Steep with boiling water for a few minutes and enjoy when cool enough. I like to add a few leaves of fresh mint, or you can sweeten it with a little sugar or agave syrup. This is also refreshing served chilled in the summer with mint and ice.

Radish, carrot and ginger salad: Made with radish roots and leaves, as well as sliced fresh ginger and carrot, this salad is peppery and a little spicy. Find the recipe on page 199.

Pickled ginger: Slices of unpeeled ginger add a nice spice to pickled vegetables. Try ginger pickled with radishes, turnips, onions or in my watermelon rind pickle recipe on pages 162–3.

Stewed or baked fruit with ginger: Try adding a few slices of ginger to stewed fruit, like apples or plums, to give the dish a kick, or incorporate this into a crumble. In my baked cinnamon apples recipe on page 13, the apples are stuffed with ginger and sultanas / golden raisins to create a sweet but spicy dessert.

Compleat Recipe: Fermented Kimchi with Turnips and Vegetables

Fermenting is a great way to preserve produce, intensify the flavour and give your gut's microbiome a boost. It has been found to enhance the available B and C vitamins, as well as aiding digestion and supporting immunity. Liz Child, chef and author of *Cook, Draw, Feed*, whose beautiful illustrations feature in this book, sparked my love of fermented foods with her easy-to-follow guides, which inspired this kimchi. In this recipe, root ginger and chilli give your kimchi a fiery and satisfying kick.

Fermenting can seem scary at first, but it's actually simple and very rewarding. We now always have a few jars of ferments on the go. They are great as a ready-made addition to any meal. It's important to ensure everything is clean when fermenting (wash produce, hands and utensils before touching), but there's no need to peel any of the vegetables or the ginger. You can also include more unusual offcuts, such as broccoli or cauliflower stalk, cabbage heart, and the ends of things like carrots, swede/rutabaga or parsnip, as well as the more commonly used parts.

Prep 30 minutes, plus fermenting time **Makes** a 1-litre/1-quart jar

- 1kg/2lb 4oz raw vegetables of your choice
- 2 tablespoons fine sea salt

Suggested vegetables:
- 2 turnips
- 2 carrots
- 1 cabbage
- 1 cauliflower

For the kimchi paste:
- 2 red chillies
- 7cm/3in piece of root ginger
- ¼ onion
- 4 garlic cloves

1   To make enough kimchi to fill a 1-litre glass jar, aim for 1kg/2lb 4oz worth of raw vegetables. This can be made up of the suggested vegetables, or from what you have to hand.

2   Thinly chop the turnips and carrots, plus any other root vegetables you'd like to include, such as swede, radishes or beetroots. No need to peel.

3   Shred the cabbage and cauliflower leaves, saving one whole large cabbage leaf to use at the end. Chop the cauliflower into small florets and slice the cauliflower stalk and cabbage heart into small chunks. If you're adding any other vegetables, then chop these into similarly sized pieces.

4   Place all of the prepared vegetables in a large bowl and add the salt. For reference, the ratio should be one tablespoon of salt to every 500g/1lb 2oz of raw vegetables. With clean hands or wearing clean gloves if you'd prefer – it can sting a little to do this – massage the salt into the vegetables for a few minutes until it starts to draw the moisture out of the produce. This is the beginning of the brine forming. Set the bowl aside whilst you make the kimchi paste.

5   Place all of the ingredients for the paste in a blender, including the seeds from the chillies. No need to peel the ginger, but the onion and garlic skins should be removed. Blitz in the blender until it forms a paste.

6   Massage the prepared vegetables once more. If you like, taste a piece. It should taste nicely salted but not unpleasant. Stir through your kimchi paste and mix well so that everything is coated. It will smell amazingly aromatic.

7   Your kimchi is now ready to be decanted into your jar(s). You want there to be as few air pockets as possible between the vegetables and for the jar to be tightly packed. As you add the vegetables, use a spoon to compress it down as much as possible and squash it into all available space in the jar.

8   Top your kimchi with a follower – this is your saved cabbage leaf. It's important that this seals the top. Think of it like a blanket to tuck all of the vegetables under. Top this with a fermenting weight or a small clean jar filled with water to keep everything weighed down.

9   Do not put the lid on your kimchi jar. Cover it with a dish towel or muslin/ cheese cloth, using a rubber band to secure it over the top so that it allows air in but not any debris. Place this on a shelf at room temperature, out of direct sunlight, and allow it to ferment for a week. It should reduce down and create a beautifully spicy taste. Ferments can be lively, so I recommend checking your kimchi daily. Check to make sure the brine has not bubbled over and to look for unwanted air pockets. If needed, hold the jar over your kitchen sink and press down on the weight to release any excess air or brine.

10 After a couple of days, taste your kimchi. It should be spicy and sour and become stronger over time so leave to ferment for a few more days if you wish. Once complete, store in a sealed jar in the fridge for up to 3 months. Be warned, fermenting can become rather addictive!

Globe artichoke

Globe artichokes are actually flowers and grow as large thistles which, if left, produce beautiful purple blooms. Whilst we often just buy the tasty artichoke heart pre-prepared in a jar or can, a little of the stalk's core and the base of each of the leaves/petals are also edible. Unfortunately, though, much of the artichoke bud can't be eaten and should be composted.

IN SEASON: June – November

MAKE IT LAST! Globe artichokes are best stored in the fridge. To preserve a batch of fresh globe artichoke hearts, first cook them (I'd recommend steaming). They can then be pickled (method on page 235) or packed into jars with olive oil, fresh herbs, garlic and lemon juice. These should be stored in the fridge and eaten within six weeks.

NUTRITIONAL BENEFITS: Globe artichokes are a good source of folate, potassium and manganese.

EDIBLE AND USEFUL PARTS: Heart, leaves/petals and stalk.

⍰ How to prepare a globe artichoke

If you've never cooked with a fresh globe artichoke then it can be rather intimidating! The easiest way is to steam the whole thing along with two garlic cloves, a slice of fresh lemon and a bay leaf. This will take roughly

45 minutes, or until the outer leaves/petals peel off easily. To get the most from the cooked artichoke, I like to then pull off all of the leaves/petals. The white base of each leaf/petal, except the really tough or very little ones, is edible. This is eaten by pulling it through your teeth to scrape the tasty flesh into your mouth – also try this with some olive oil or a dip. Once the leaves/petals are removed, in the very centre you will find the flower-like parts with purple leaves/petals and the furry choke. These are definitely not edible so twist off those (and compost them) until you find the soft and delicious heart hidden beneath. This is great as is, grilled or on top of pizza, pasta, salad or bruschetta. The heart continues down into the centre of the stalk for a few centimetres, so this can also be peeled to find the soft and tasty flesh.

Globe artichoke leaf/petal stock: Prepare your artichokes as above. Sadly, it's only a small part of each leaf/petal which can be eaten. Save the wasted part of the leaves/petals and simmer them in a saucepan of boiling water for 45 minutes to create a unique-tasting broth. Strain out and compost the leaves/petals. The cooled water can be saved in a jar in the fridge for up to a week and used in place of stock in dishes like soup or risotto.

Herbs

Fresh herbs are amazingly aromatic and a joy to cook with. Herbs like rosemary, sage and mint are hardy and grow well outdoors, whilst herbs like basil, coriander/cilantro and parsley can bring some edible greenery to your windowsill year-round. For most herbs, the leaves, stalks and flowers can all be added to dishes.

MAKE IT LAST! Most cut herbs should be stored in the fridge. To help keep a bunch fresh, stand it in a glass of water in the fridge. You could also chop and freeze fresh herbs, ready to add directly to soups, stews and sauces.

EDIBLE AND USEFUL PARTS: Leaves, stalks and flowers.

🗎 Leaves

Herb leaves hold the key to flavour in our kitchens. Chop the entire leaves, and often the stalks too, through dishes. As a guide, one tablespoon of fresh herbs equates to one teaspoon of dried. Some of my favourite herby recipes include parsley in a puttanesca pasta sauce (pages 223–4), coriander/cilantro scattered over ramen (pages 53–5) and roasted sage and butternut squash ravioli (pages 88–90).

🌿 Stalks

The stalks from most herbs can be chopped and added to dishes, just as you would the leaves. This is great for delicate herbs like basil, mint, coriander and parsley. However, you might prefer to compost or make a broth from more woody herb stalks, such as rosemary.

Offcuts broth: Along with offcuts from vegetables, I like to freeze the very hard stalks from herbs like rosemary or sage, which are usually too woody to eat. Save these and simmer them as part of a flavoursome stock. Turn to pages 232–4 for the recipe.

❀ Flowers

Fresh herbs are great grown in a garden or on a windowsill. However, after some time, most will flower. This means that the plant is no longer putting energy into growing tasty leaves and all its efforts are going into the flowers and it could go to seed. A simple solution is to snip off all of the flowers. The flowers are edible and taste much like the leaves. Add them to dishes as you would the rest of the herb. For example, brew a fresh mint flower tea, or add oregano and basil flowers to a roasted tomato pasta sauce.

☑ My favourite ways to compleat:

Herb-infused olive oil: Use fresh sprigs of herbs like rosemary, basil or sage to infuse a bottle or jar of olive oil. Turn to pages 236–7 for the recipe. Infused oils are delicious as a dressing for salads, pastas and other dishes, or great as a gift for friends.

Fresh herbal teas: Steep a few leaves, stalks (and flowers if you need to use them) of your fresh herb of choice in a strainer over a mug of boiled water for around five minutes. Fresh mint, lemon balm, lavender, lemon verbena, fennel or chamomile all make a delicious packaging-free brew. The leaves could also be saved and dried to have a year-round supply of tea.

My favourite tips to use up fresh herbs:

• **Carrot and coriander/cilantro soup:** If a bunch of coriander is past its best, use it up by blending it into a homemade carrot and coriander soup.

• **Roasted tomato, basil and oregano sauce:** Roast fresh tomatoes with a few cloves of garlic and generous amounts of fresh oregano and basil, tossed in olive oil to make your own, flavour-filled sauce to enjoy with pasta or on pizza. Turn to the tomatoes chapter for the full recipe (page 222).

• **Frozen herby flavour cubes:** Chop fresh herbs, such as basil, rosemary, oregano or thyme, as well as optional garlic. Sprinkle generously into ice cube trays and fill with olive oil. Freeze and add to dishes as and when needed for a ready-made hit of herby flavour.

• **Homemade mint sauce:** It's not quite traditional, but I love to serve this with roasted vegetables and savoury pies. Chop one bunch of fresh mint (leaves and stalks) into small pieces. Mix in a bowl with a pinch of salt and one tablespoon sugar. Pour over three tablespoons boiled water and set aside to cool. Once cooled, mix in three tablespoons white wine vinegar and taste. Add more water, vinegar or mint to strengthen or dilute the sauce. Store in a jar in the fridge and eat within a few weeks.

• **Mint and berry ice cubes:** In an ice cube tray, place a few leaves of mint, plus any berries which might need using up (raspberries work well) into each hole. Fill with water and freeze. Once frozen, add to drinks and cocktails.

🌿 How to dry herbs

This is best done at the end of summer to allow the plant to flourish in the warm months and give you a supply of herbs over winter. Take cuttings from the herb you want to dry, making sure you still leave enough for the plant to recover – don't take more than one third of the plant at once. Bundle the cuttings into bunches of five to ten small branches with leaves. Tie each bunch at the base with string to secure, allowing some extra string at the end for hanging. Hang the bunches to dry somewhere that is covered but with a flow of fresh air. For example, a conservatory, out building or well-ventilated hallway. Drying time varies from herb to herb and could take between a few weeks and a few months. Once dried, store the herbs in a jar for up to a year. It's worth noting that whilst this does work for all herbs, those with more moisture, such as basil, can take a long time to dry so freezing can be an easier method of preserving its flavour.

🌱 Green-fingered ideas

I have large rosemary and sage plants in our garden and have propagated them to grow new plants for friends and family. This can be achieved with most woody herbs. To do so, tear off a small branch from the main stem of the herb, making sure you include some of the heel from the main stem. Take four to five pieces so that you have backups if one doesn't survive. Remove any leaves near the bottom of the cuttings. Plant them around the edges of a small pot filled with well-watered compost. Make sure that the compost stays moist. Some of the leaves may die off but with some love, a new plant will gradually start to grow over the next few weeks or months.

Jackfruit

Jackfruit is a large fruit grown on trees and commonly found across Asia, Africa and tropical climates. It has recently soared in popularity across the world. It is sold in two forms – young and unripe or mature and ripe. The unripe fruit is used in dishes like curries and burgers due to its meaty texture and ability to absorb flavours. Ripe jackfruit is used in desserts and is deliciously sweet. Fresh jackfruit can be sourced on the internet, and may soon be available worldwide.

IN SEASON: Jackfruit is available year-round. It's worth considering the carbon footprint of tropical fruits.

MAKE IT LAST! Jackfruit is most commonly sold in cans which should be stored at room temperature. Prepared or fresh jackfruit should be stored in the fridge or frozen. Fresh jackfruit continues to ripen upon resting so prepare it as soon as possible once it reaches your desired maturity.

NUTRITIONAL BENEFITS: Jackfruit is a great source of protein, as well as calcium, iron and vitamins A and C.

EDIBLE AND USEFUL PARTS: Flesh, seeds and core.

⊡ Flesh

Jackfruit flesh is really versatile and absorbs flavours so works especially well in spicy dishes like curry or a smoky chilli. Also try "pulling" the flesh and coating it in a barbeque sauce – perfect for topping pizzas, burgers or nachos.

⊞ Seeds

If you source a fresh jackfruit, it can be quite laborious to prepare but yields lots of flesh. However, the seeds are also edible and are a source of protein. Roast the seeds, as you would with pumpkin seeds, and eat them as snacks or with salads. They have a nutty taste.

⊟ Core

Jackfruit core is also edible, and often found in cans of jackfruit, as well as in the fresh fruit. It has a slightly tougher texture than the flesh but can be shredded with a knife and cooked with the rest of the fruit.

• **Also try these alternatives to jackfruit:** You can achieve a similar effect to pulled jackfruit using leftover banana peels. Find my recipe on pages 28-9, where the pulled peels are marinated in a barbeque sauce. Spaghetti squash is another amazing vegetable, which naturally has a pulled, spaghetti-like texture. Try using it to make burgers, in curries or as a pasta replacement.

Kale

Hailed as a superfood, kale is full of important vitamins and minerals. As well as the more common green curly kale, also try purple kale and cavalo nero, which originates from Tuscany but is now grown in the UK. All types of kale can be compleated, making the most of the whole leaves and stalk.

IN SEASON: September – April

MAKE IT LAST! Kale is best stored in the fridge and can also be chopped and frozen to add to dishes like curries, dahl, soups and stews.

NUTRITIONAL BENEFITS:
The leaves and stalk of kale are brimming with vitamins A, C, K and iron, as well as being a great source of fibre and calcium, a mineral that's important for healthy teeth, bones, muscles and blood. Kale is also a good plant-based source of alpha-linolenic acid, or ALA, which is a type of omega-3 fatty acid.

EDIBLE AND USEFUL PARTS:
Leaves and stalks.

🌿 Leaves

Kale leaves are so versatile – delicious lightly fried with some garlic and enjoyed on toast or added to a variety of dishes. Try using the leaves as an alternative to basil or spinach in pesto (recipe on page 158) or to add some extra flavour to a cauliflower cheeze (pages 72–3). I especially love eating brassicas like kale raw in a salad with toppings like tomatoes, seeds and courgette/zucchini ribbons.

🌱 Stalk

So many recipes tell you to discard the stalk and any harder parts of kale, but there's really no need. I love cooking with the stalks because they add a nice mix of textures to dishes. Try chopping it through a stir-fry, salad, curry, stew or ramen and use as you would the kale leaves, or shredded into a coleslaw (recipe on pags 63–4). If the stalk is especially tough, chop into chunks and add to a fermented kimchi (recipe on pags 133–5).

☑ My favourite ways to compleat:

Compleat cauliflower cheeze with kale: My recipe for a creamy cauliflower cheeze uses the whole cauliflower and is baked with chopped kale stalk and leaves. A satisfying and compleat comfort dish! See pages 72-3 for the recipe.

Crispy seaweed-style kale: If you're a fan of crispy seaweed - the type you buy from a takeaway - then you'll love this. You'll need around 80g/2¾oz of kale and can use both the leaves and stalks. Shred the leaves very thinly and chop the stalks into small thin strips. In a bowl, mix the kale with two teaspoons sesame oil, one teaspoon sesame seeds, one teaspoon brown sugar and ½ teaspoon sea salt so that it is evenly coated. Spread out on a baking tray and cook at 180°C/350°F/gas mark 4 for seven to nine minutes, checking and mixing regularly so that it cooks evenly to a crispy but not burned texture.

Stir-fried offcut greens: I love the simplicity of stir-fried greens – cook with slices of garlic and sesame oil and it's effortlessly tasty. You can incorporate chopped kale and broccoli stalks and cauliflower or sprout leaves for a different take on traditional greens.

Pici pasta: This type of pasta is so easy to make using flour and greens. It is rolled by hand and cooks quickly. My recipe on pages 201–2 uses spinach and green beans but these can be switched for or supplemented with kale.

• **A note about veggie offcuts broth:** Whilst most vegetable offcuts are delicious added to a broth (pages 232–4), be aware that brassicas like kale can cause your broth to taste bitter so add these sparingly if at all.

Compleat Recipe: Coconutty Kale and Chickpea Dahl

Full of flavour and goodness, my dahl recipe uses the stalks and leaves of a big bunch of kale. Fresh coconut really tops it off, and you can make your own coconut milk and shavings, but this is still tasty if using shop bought. Serve with rice or bread or as part of a thali.

Prep 10 minutes **Cooking** 30 minutes
Serves 4 as a main with rice or bread

• 1 teaspoon coconut oil
• 1 white onion, diced
• 2 cloves garlic, finely chopped
• 2.5cm/1in piece of root ginger
• 1 teaspoon cumin seeds
• ½ teaspoon ground turmeric
• 2 teaspoons curry powder
• Around 200g/7oz kale (leaves and stalks)
• 400g/14oz can of chickpeas/ garbanzo beans

- 400ml/14fl oz/1¾ cups coconut milk (canned or make your own, recipe on pages 107–8)
- 100g/3½oz/heaped ½ cup dried red lentils
- 2 teaspoons mango chutney
- Handful of fresh coconut shavings (optional but really delicious, see page 108 for how to prepare)
- Salt and black pepper
- Rice or bread, to serve

1 Heat the coconut oil in a large saucepan with a lid over a low to medium heat. Add the onion and after a few minutes add the garlic. (The onion and garlic skins can be saved to make a broth if you wish, pages 232–4.) Grate in the root ginger, including the skin. After 2 minutes, add the cumin seeds, turmeric and curry powder. Mix well.

2 Chop the kale leaves and stalks into even pieces and mix into the pan. Season with salt and pepper. Drain the chickpeas and save the aquafaba for another recipe if you wish (see pages 86–8). After 2 minutes, add the chickpeas and mix well. Pour in the coconut milk and increase the heat a little to achieve a simmer.

3 Stir in the red lentils and mango chutney. Cover with a lid and simmer for 15–20 minutes, stirring occasionally, until the lentils are cooked. Remove from the heat and serve in bowls with rice or bread and top with coconut shavings.

Kiwi

Most of us probably peel a kiwi without thinking but there's actually a lot of goodness in that outer shell. Whilst a kiwi can be eaten whole and raw, like an apple, the experience is a little furry! But blended into a smoothie, juice or sauce, the kiwi is a waste-free winner.

IN SEASON: At its best in spring and summer. It's also worth considering the carbon footprint of tropical fruits like this.

MAKE IT LAST! Keep at room temperature until ripe. Once ripe, store in the fridge. You could also freeze any leftover slices to add to drinks and cocktails or smoothies.

NUTRITIONAL BENEFITS: Kiwi fruits are rich in vitamin C, especially when eaten raw – great for boosting immunity and overall health. The skin is packed with fibre and antioxidants.

EDIBLE AND USEFUL PARTS: Flesh, skin and seeds.

Flesh

Refreshing as a snack or added to desserts, fruit salads, salsa, smoothies, juices and jam. Eat the sweet green flesh complete with the tiny seeds.

⏏ Skin

Packed with fibre, save any kiwi skin peelings to blend into smoothies and juices or chop sparingly in thin slices through salads.

☑ My favourite ways to compleat:

Smoothies and juices: Kiwi flesh and skin can be blended into smoothies and juices. The flavour works well with lime juice and apple.

Dried kiwi slices: Cut the kiwi into slices, as thinly as possible, leaving the skin on. Spread evenly on a baking tray and cook at 100°C/200°F/gas mark ½ for two to three hours, until fully dried. Eat as a snack or topping for smoothie bowls, granola (pages 238-9) and desserts. Follow this same process with different fruits, like apricots and mango, and ideally bake one big batch of dried fruits at once. Store in a jar for up to a month.

Kiwi ice lollies: Blend your kiwis, including the skin, and add a little water or apple juice to reach the desired consistency. Pour into ice cube trays or ice lolly moulds. Freeze overnight and enjoy. You could also add layers of blended watermelon, mango or pineapple.

Compleat Recipe: Duo of Salsas with Baked Kiwi and Pineapple Core

I love Mexican food because you can create so much flavour without any need to top it with cheese or dairy. Using the whole kiwi – including the skin – and a leftover pineapple core, my duo of salsas is sweet but fiery. Try these drizzled over fajitas, as topping for tacos or as a dip with tortilla chips. You could even make your own chips from leftover or stale tortilla wraps (pages 43–4).

Prep 20 minutes

Cooking 30 minutes

Makes 2 generous bowls of salsa

For the kiwi salsa verde:
- 1 kiwi, sliced in half with skin on
- 1 medium salad tomato, sliced in half
- 1 garlic clove, peeled
- Handful of fresh coriander/cilantro leaves and stalks, chopped
- Juice of ½ lime
- 2.5cm/1in piece of fresh red chilli, diced
- Salt and black pepper

For the pineapple core pico de gallo:
- 1 pineapple core from a used pineapple
- Coconut oil, for brushing
- ¼ red pepper, diced
- ¼ small red onion, diced
- 2.5cm/1in piece of fresh red chilli, finely chopped
- Handful of fresh coriander/cilantro leaves and stalks, chopped
- Juice of ½ lime
- Salt and black pepper

To serve:
- Tortilla chips, fajitas or tacos

1 Place the kiwi halves (skin on) and tomato halves in an ovenproof dish. Add the pineapple core and brush it with a little coconut oil to prevent it from drying out. Bake in the oven at 180°C/350°F/gas mark 4.

2 After 10 minutes, remove the tomato halves from the dish and return the rest to the oven. Cook for a further 10 minutes, then remove the kiwi halves from the oven and set aside. Allow the pineapple core to bake for a further 10 minutes until softened. Remove from the oven and set aside.

3 To make the kiwi salsa verde, place the kiwi and tomato in a bowl with the garlic clove, coriander, lime juice and chilli. Season well with salt and pepper. Blend the mix using a hand blender until smooth. Taste and adjust spice and seasoning as desired. It should be sweet but with a spicy kick.

4 To make the pineapple core pico de gallo, chop the baked core into small chunks. Mix in a bowl with the red pepper, onion, chilli, coriander and lime juice. Season with salt and pepper and adjust spice levels as desired.

5 Serve with tortilla chips (pages 43–4), fajitas or tacos.

Leek

Despite being part of the same family as onions and garlic, leeks are often overlooked. But cook them well and make use of the whole plant and you won't look at leeks the same way again. The green leafy top that we often discard is possibly the tastiest part! Use the whole leek in soups, stews, pies and tarts or in place of onion in a vegetable risotto.

IN SEASON: September – March

MAKE IT LAST! Leeks are best stored in the fridge. They can also be sliced and frozen, ready to add to dishes. When cleaning your leek, slice it lengthways down the middle, and wash the two halves under cold running water so that there's no need to discard any muddy or green parts.

NUTRITIONAL BENEFITS: Leeks are an excellent source of vitamins A, B6 and K, as well as containing manganese and some vitamin C. The green leafy tops of your leeks are just as healthy and tasty as the white part.

EDIBLE AND USEFUL PARTS: Flesh, leaves and roots.

Leafy top

The leafy green top of a leek and the outer leaves that we commonly slice off and discard are actually full of flavour. They might take slightly longer to cook but are so worth compleating. Chop these through dishes like risotto, stew and soup, as you would with the white of the leek. You could also separate, shred and sauté them to top dishes like soup or to mix into mashed potatoes as a colcannon (pages 185–6). If you don't fancy adding it to a dish, the green leek top can also be boiled with vegetable offcuts to make a broth (pages 232–4).

Sautéed leek greens: These are great as a side or garnish. Thinly shred the leek top and sauté it in a frying pan with one tablespoon of plant butter for a few minutes until slightly softened. This part of the leek is especially flavoursome, but you could add a little salt and pepper or garlic if you wish.

⊞ Roots

The stringy roots on the end of a leek are edible and packed full of a surprising amount of flavour. They taste a bit like fresh chives or little spring onions/scallions, just make sure you clean them well. Sadly they are usually removed from shop-bought leeks but are a delight if you grow your own. The roots are tasty raw as a garnish and can also be chopped and cooked into dishes with the rest of the leek. Try them sautéed in a little butter as a topping for soup or risotto.

☑ My favourite ways to compleat:

Braised leeks: These creamy braised leeks use the whole leek, plus roots and green top and are great as a tasty side. Slice one leek lengthways down the middle and wash the two halves under cold running water to clean before slicing the entire leek thinly. Melt two tablespoons of plant butter in a sauté pan, add the leeks and cover with a lid. Leave the leeks to sweat down for two to three minutes, then stir in two tablespoons nutritional yeast and one teaspoon miso paste. Mix well and season with salt and pepper to taste.

Root vegetable and leek gratin: Chop a whole leek or two through a creamy baked vegetable gratin in place of onion. For my celeriac gratin recipe, see pages 77–8, and add whichever root vegetables you wish.

▦ Odds and ends

Offcuts broth: Along with other vegetable offcuts, freeze the cleaned leek roots and any green leek tops that you might not have used in a tub and save to make stock (see my recipe on page 232-4)

Compleat Recipe: Celeriac, Leek and Potato Soup, Topped with Sautéed Leek Greens

Most leek soup recipes ask you to discard the outer leaves, leafy top and roots from the leek. However, these are just as tasty as the white of the leek and, when sautéed, add extra goodness and texture to the soup. If you prefer traditional leek and potato soup, then omit the celeriac and use two to three medium potatoes. An appetising and waste-free take on a classic soup.

Prep 15 minutes **Cooking** 45 minutes
Serves 4

- 2 medium leeks
- 1 tablespoon rapeseed/canola oil
- 3 garlic cloves

- 1 medium unpeeled potato
- 1 medium unpeeled whole celeriac
- 800ml/28fl oz/3½ cups stock
- 150ml/5fl oz/scant 2/3 cup oat milk
- 1 tablespoon plant butter
- Salt and black pepper

1   Slice the leeks down their length into halves and rinse well under cold running water. Separate off the darker green tops and any roots and reserve those for cooking at the end as a garnish. Often, the centre of the green leek top is white and soft. If so, that can be separated to cook along with the rest of the leek flesh. Thinly slice the leek flesh.

2   Heat the rapeseed/canola oil in a large saucepan over a medium to low heat. Add the leeks and cover with a lid to allow to sweat for 5–7 minutes until cooked down. Meanwhile, dice the garlic cloves and cube the potato and celeriac. There's no need to peel these. When preparing the celeriac, chop and rinse the roots especially well. They may look strange but are just as flavoursome as the rest of the vegetable.

3   Add the diced garlic to the pan and mix well. After a few minutes, add the chopped potato and celeriac. Mix and pour in the stock. Bring to the boil, cover and simmer for around 30 minutes or until the root vegetables are softened.

4   Remove from the heat, add the oat milk and blend using a hand blender. Taste and season with a little salt and pepper. You may wish to be more generous with the salt if you are using homemade stock. Set the soup to one side whilst you prepare the leek greens.

5   Thinly shred the saved green leek leaves and roots. Heat the butter in a frying pan over a medium heat and add these. Mix and sauté for a few minutes until softened but still with a little bite. Remove from the heat.

6   Serve the warm soup in bowls, topped with the sautéed leek greens.

▦ Green-fingered ideas

You can experiment with planting an offcut root end of a leek. Save a 5cm/2in piece and cook with the rest of the leek as you wish. Stand the leek piece, roots down, in a saucer with enough water to cover the roots. Place on your windowsill for up to a week, until the roots begin to grow and new green growth shoots upwards from the leek. Change the water regularly and be careful not to let it get mouldy. Once a leek plant is established, after a week or two, plant it in a pot with moist soil so that the roots are buried, and the green top is above the surface. If any of the old white leek flesh looks to be rotting, remove and compost this before planting. Keep the leek plant in a sunny spot and water regularly. The leek will keep sprouting and can be harvested when you're happy with its size.

Lettuce (and salad bags)

The whole lettuce is edible – including the harder stalk, core and stems found in some varieties. So often, lettuces and bags of salad, like rocket/arugula, lamb's lettuce, baby leaves or watercress, are left unloved to go limp in the fridge. But there's much more you can create with these than just salad. Try making lettuce leaf tacos or serve your whole lettuce warm and charred over a griddle pan. Older lettuce or salad leaves need not go to waste – they can be blended into a soup, smoothies or pesto.

IN SEASON: May – December

MAKE IT LAST! Lettuces are best stored in the fridge. Smaller varieties, like leaf lettuce or Romaine, can also be stood root-down in a jar with a little water to help keep them fresh.

NUTRITIONAL BENEFITS: Lettuces are a great source of vitamin K, which helps blood clot to heal wounds. Each lettuce variety has its own nutritional benefits, including different minerals and a high hydrating water content. Iceberg, for example, boasts vitamins A, C and K, as well as calcium, potassium and folate.

EDIBLE AND USEFUL PARTS: Leaves, core and stalks.

🌿 Leaves

Great in a salad on a warm day, lettuce is hydrating and more versatile than you might think.

Try topping your salad with toasted seeds and nuts to add a nutritious crunch, or enjoy your lettuce warm.

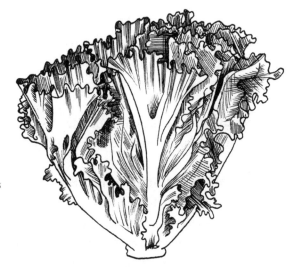

Lettuce leaf tacos:
Substitute flour tortilla wraps for lettuce leaves and fill them with cooked spicy lentils, tofu or vegetables. In place of wraps, the leaves are pleasantly light and refreshing and balance out any heat from chilli. Try them topped with homemade pickled onions.

☑ My favourite ways to compleat:

Griddled or barbequed lettuce wedges: This works well with smaller lettuce varieties, such as the Little Gem/Bibb lettuce. Slice your whole lettuce into two to four wedges and drizzle with olive oil. Cook over the barbeque or in a griddle pan over a high heat for a few minutes each side. Some char marks are great and add to the cooked flavour. Serve as a side, with a burger or added to a salad. Also try drizzling over a little balsamic vinegar once cooked.

Pasta salads: Shred and toss the lettuce leaves through a pasta salad with olive oil, salt, pepper, herbs, tomatoes, olives and raw vegetables. The harder parts of the lettuce, like the heart or stems, can also be diced and stirred through.

Soups: Lettuce leaves, as well as the harder parts, can be blended into soups, such as a pea, mint and lettuce soup. If you just want to use up the stalk, then diced and blended in a soup is a good option.

Smoothies: All parts of a lettuce can be added to smoothies or juices, whether to use up the lettuce or give the drink an extra boost.

Compleat Recipe: Salad Bag Greens Pesto

Bags of pre-packed salad leaves are often sold in the reduced section of the supermarket as soon as they get close to their "best before" date. At full price, I try to avoid buying these. However, if you already have a bag wilting in the fridge – or, like me, can't resist saving reduced goods from going to waste – these are perfect for whipping into a pesto sauce. This sauce is flavoursome, light and there's no Parmesan in sight. Stir your pesto through pasta, enjoy on crackers or use to top a pizza or tart.

Prep 5 minutes
Serves 4 as a main with pasta

- 140g/5oz salad leaves (from a salad bag or mixed yourself, using a combination of lettuce, spinach, beetroot leaves, rocket/arugula or watercress)
- 30g/1oz fresh basil (optional)
- 2 garlic cloves
- 6 tablespoons nuts (pine nuts or walnuts work well)
- 6 tablespoons olive oil, plus extra if needed
- 4 tablespoons nutritional yeast, plus extra if needed
- 2 tablespoons lemon juice, plus extra if needed
- 1 teaspoon salt

1   Place everything in a food processor and add two tablespoons water. You can include the skin from the garlic, as well as the clove. Chop or break up the nuts a little before adding those.

2 Blend well on a high speed until everything is very finely chopped and blended. Remove the lid from the food processor to check everything is well combined and use a spoon to move the contents around before blending again if needed. This achieves a traditional rough pesto. You can also try this in a blender for a smooth sauce.

3 Taste the pesto and add more oil, lemon juice or nutritional yeast if you think it needs it. Serve immediately or store in a sealed jar in the fridge for a few days. Delicious and waste-free. This is also perfect for freezing in portions, ready to defrost and stir through pasta. Delicious and waste-free.

🪴 Green-fingered ideas

Lettuce offcuts are fairly easy to use to regrow a small lettuce. To do so, save a 2cm/¾in piece from the root end of your lettuce. Rest it in a saucer with a little water, using cocktail sticks to stand it upright if needed. Place on your windowsill and it will quickly begin to grow a new mini lettuce out of the top of the offcut. Change the water regularly and be careful not to let it get mouldy. The new lettuce can be harvested and eaten as normal. Take care and it will regrow time and time again. If your plant becomes well established, it can be transferred to a pot with compost to allow it to grow further.

Melon

Although it's the melon
flesh we usually head
for, the seeds and rind
are edible and tasty. This
chapter mainly features
watermelon – for which
the recipes work best
– but you can use any
melon in its place, such as
cantaloupe or honeydew.

IN SEASON: Melons are at their best during summer. It's also worth considering the carbon footprint of tropical fruits like this.

MAKE IT LAST! Whole melons are best stored at room temperature. Once chopped, store in the fridge. The chopped flesh can also be frozen, ready to add to a smoothie, juice or sorbet.

NUTRITIONAL BENEFITS: Melons contain around 90 per cent water so are great for hydration. They are a good source of vitamins A and C. Watermelon is also a source of vitamin B6 and the seeds are high in fibre, protein, iron, magnesium, potassium and vitamins.

EDIBLE AND USEFUL PARTS: Flesh, rind and seeds.

⌗ Flesh

Fresh melon on a hot day is so refreshing. Enjoy in salads, juices, smoothies or chopped into chunks. Try my watermelon sorbet recipe which is perfect for summer.

Easy watermelon sorbet: Freeze the cubed flesh of a watermelon for around eight hours. You'll need roughly half a cup per person. To serve four people, add two cups of frozen watermelon cubes to a food processor with the juice of half a lime and one teaspoon of sweetener, like agave or golden syrup. Blitz for 30 seconds, adjust lime and sweetener to taste, and serve immediately.

⌗ Seeds

All melon seeds are edible when prepared correctly, but the watermelon, honeydew and cantaloupe seeds are most popular. They are rich in vitamins and minerals. Try sprouting the seeds to capture their goodness; or toast and husk to create a nutritious snack.

Toasted seeds: Separate and rinse the seeds of any melon. Dry and coat in a little oil and season with salt. You could also experiment with other flavourings, like chilli powder or ground cinnamon. Spread evenly on a baking tray and cook in the oven at 180°C/350°F/gas mark 4 for five to ten minutes, checking the seeds don't burn. Enjoy the seeds as a snack or add to salads, granola, homemade cereal bars, flapjacks or energy balls.

Depending on the size and variety of your seeds, you may want to husk them. This is most likely the case with a watermelon so, after toasting, remove the hard, dark shell and eat the softer white insides.

⌗ Rind

When we prepare a melon, we usually eat the juicy flesh but miss out on the rind – leaving it attached to the harder skin. However, the rind (the firmer, light green coloured part between the flesh and the skin) is edible. Save it to blend into juices and smoothies, as you would the flesh. Also try chopping it into a salad or cooking small chunks in a curry alongside other vegetables.

Infuse drinks: Save the fresh rind and add to drinks to infuse a subtle taste. It's especially refreshing sliced into iced water with fresh mint and allowed to infuse for a few hours before drinking.

Sweet watermelon rind chutney: "Waatlemoen konfyt" is a traditional preserve made in South Africa using watermelon rinds. It is sweet and fragrant. To make, soak 300g/10½oz of chopped watermelon rind in salted water overnight. When ready, strain. In a saucepan, dissolve 300g/10½oz sugar into 200ml/7fl oz/scant 1 cup water. Bring to the boil. Add the watermelon rind, juice of one lemon, 1cm/½in of sliced root ginger (skin on), one teaspoon ground cinnamon and ½ teaspoon ground nutmeg. Simmer on a medium heat for 35–40 minutes until a syrup forms. Pour into a sterilized jar.

Blend into smoothies or juice: Use the rind alongside or in place of melon flesh and blend into smoothies and juices.

Pickled Watermelon Rind

This recipe makes use of the watermelon rind – that's the firm light green bit between the hard skin and pink flesh. A little flesh can be left attached but remove all of the hard, dark green skin. The texture and taste of the rind are quite different to that of the watermelon's flesh. Pickled with ginger and chilli, it's fiery but sweet. (Recipe over the page.)

Prep 30 minutes. **Cooking** 10 minutes
Makes enough for 1 700ml jar

- 400g/14oz watermelon rind
- 100ml/3½fl oz/scant ½ cup vinegar of your choice (apple cider or white wine vinegars work well)
- 1 tablespoon salt
- 1 fresh red chilli, sliced (keep seeds)
- 2.5cm/1in piece of root ginger, unpeeled and finely sliced
- ½ teaspoon coriander seeds
- ½ teaspoon mustard seeds

1 Separate the watermelon rind by removing the peel and slicing off the flesh. Compost the peel and reserve the flesh for another recipe. Chop the rind into even chunks, about 5mm/¼in thick.

2 In a saucepan, combine the vinegar, salt, red chilli, root ginger and 270ml/9½fl oz/scant 1¼ cups water. Bring to the boil. Once boiling, add the chopped rind. Simmer for 5 minutes. Turn off the heat and stir through the coriander and mustard seeds.

3 Sterilize your jar (see page 232) and carefully add the contents of the pan whilst still hot. It is ready to eat once cooled and will infuse further upon standing. Store for a month in the fridge.

▦ Green-fingered ideas

Melon seeds can be saved to plant. Wash your fresh seeds in a fine-mesh sieve/strainer under a tap to rinse off any juice or pulp until they are completely clean. Spread the seeds on a plate on an absorbent layer (like a paper towel) to soak up the moisture and leave them in a warm cupboard for a few weeks until completely dry. You can then store them in an envelope to sow in spring.

▣ Green pet foods

As a child, I always fed any melon rinds to our pet guinea pigs. Fed sparingly, they are a lovely treat and great for extra hydration on a hot day.

Mushrooms

Mushroom peelers ... please step away from the knife! There's no need to peel or top and tail fresh mushrooms, you can happily rinse and compleat them. Any mushrooms that might be a little wrinkly or past their best can be simmered into dishes like vegetable bolognaise or a stew, or to create a tasty mushroom broth. Mushrooms are a delicious addition to a vegetable risotto and are great sautéed in sesame oil and added to a ramen (recipe on page 53).

IN SEASON: September – November

MAKE IT LAST! Mushrooms are best stored in the fridge. You can also slice and freeze them, ready to add to dishes.

NUTRITIONAL BENEFITS: Mushrooms are a great source of B vitamins. They also contain the antioxidant selenium, which helps to support the immune system and prevent cell and tissue damage.

Mushrooms were named as part of the "clean 15" in recent research. This means that they were found to contain little, if any, pesticide residues!

EDIBLE AND USEFUL PARTS: Flesh and skin.

☑ My favourite ways to compleat:

Mushroom broth: Past-their-best mushrooms are perfect for simmering into soups or broths. A homemade mushroom broth can be used as a base for dishes like ramen or risotto. To make yours, simmer a handful of mushrooms in a large saucepan of water for 45 minutes. You could also include some vegetable scraps, such as onion or garlic skins or root vegetable peelings. When ready, the broth will be dark in colour and rich in flavour. Strain out and compost any vegetable scraps. If you're making a soup, include the mushrooms. If you want to save this broth to use later, allow it to cool before decanting into airtight jars and in the fridge for up to a week.

Dried mushrooms: Drying is a great way to preserve lots of mushrooms, useful if you forage or have purchased a large amount. Mushrooms can be dried in a dehydrator or oven. If using an oven, wash, slice and dry your mushrooms of any excess water. Spread the slices evenly on a baking tray and cook for two to three hours on your oven's lowest temperature, turning and checking them every hour. Once fully dried, allow to cool and store in an airtight jar for up to a year. When you want to cook with the mushrooms, soak them in a bowl with boiled water for 30 minutes before straining and cooking as normal. The liquid from soaking will be flavoursome and can be added to soups and broths.

Oats

This chapter focuses on using oats to make homemade oat milk. Oat milk is quick and easy to make and, if you buy your oats plastic-free or from a zero-waste shop, you can avoid excess packaging. Also try using oats to make your own granola, recipe on pages 238–9.

MAKE IT LAST! Oats should be stored in an airtight container at room temperature, such as a jar.

NUTRITIONAL BENEFITS: Oats are high in fibre and provide useful slow-release energy. They also contain manganese, selenium, phosphorus, thiamine and magnesium.

EDIBLE AND USEFUL PARTS: Oats and pulp.

How to make oat milk: Pour 80g/3oz/¾ cup rolled oats into a blender with 1l/35fl oz/4¼ cups water. Blend for one minute to create the milk. Pour through a nut milk bag or very fine mesh strainer over a jug to strain the milk out and collect the oat pulp. Squeeze the pulp so that all of the milk is strained out. Add an optional pinch of salt or a little sweetener, such as agave syrup, to taste. Decant the milk into a glass bottle and store in the fridge for up to five days. Shake before using. Save the oat pulp to use as follows.

How to use oat pulp: The leftover pulp from making oat milk is full of goodness so don't discard it. Add the pulp to smoothies, porridge, granola and overnight oats or mix a little into bread dough. It can also be transformed into oat cookies, flapjacks, crackers, the topping for a fruit crumble or an exfoliating a face mask.

Waste-free oat pulp crackers: In a bowl, mix the oat pulp from making milk (roughly four tablespoons' worth). Add 70g/2½oz/2/3 cup rolled oats. If you have more oat pulp leftover from making milk then you can supplement the rolled oats with this. Mix in ¼ teaspoon salt and one tablespoon seeds of your choice. I like to use pumpkin, poppy, chia and sunflower seeds. Mix well and add two tablespoons plant butter. Pour in 125ml/4fl oz/½ cup warm water. Mix well and spread onto a baking tray lined with greaseproof paper. Spread the mix as thinly as possible, using a spoon or your hands to squash it out into one large cracker. Bake in the oven at 190°C/375°F/gas mark 5 for 30 minutes. Remove from the oven and allow to cool before slicing into cracker squares. Store in an airtight container and eat within a few days.

Onions and spring onions/scallions

The humble onion is key to so many dishes, featuring in our cooking every day, but discarding the papery outer skin results in a lot of waste. This part is actually really useful in broths and to boost nutrition, as well as in the garden. Whenever I'm cooking, onion skins and other offcuts go straight into a freezer bag, ready for making stock. It's a simple but satisfying way to repurpose your waste.

IN SEASON: Year-round

MAKE IT LAST! Store onions in a cool, dry place like a cupboard or cloth bag. If you only use half, wrap and store the leftover half in the fridge; or chop and freeze it ready to cook from frozen. Pickling and fermenting are useful ways to preserve onions for longer, especially if you grow your own.

NUTRITIONAL BENEFITS: Onions are rich in vitamin C and are a source of fibre and folate. Interestingly, the skins we usually throw away have anti-inflammatory properties. Research has found that when ground dry onion skins are added to bread dough it significantly boosts the quercetin, giving the bread antioxidant and anti-inflammatory benefits.[1]

1 Urszula Gawlik-Dziki et al, "Quality and antioxidant properties of breads enriched with dry onion skin", *ScienceDirect*, 2013.

Onions were named as part of the "clean 15" in recent research. This means that they were found to contain little, if any, pesticide residues!

EDIBLE AND USEFUL PARTS: Flesh, skin and spring onion roots.

⬚ Flesh

We all use the flesh of onions, but did you know its health benefits are more potent when eaten raw? And to reduce waste when preparing your onion for cooking, nip off just the very end of the root and tip before slicing.

Pickled onions: Pickling is a great way to preserve many veggies, like onions. I often have a jar on the go in the fridge. You can use the vinegar from shop-bought jars or make your own with your choice of vinegar infused with a garlic clove and a little sugar and salt. See page 235 for my easy pickling recipe. I especially like to pickle the bits of flesh you might prefer not to cook with, such as the harder layers of the onion and the top of the bulb.

Roasted whole onion: Roast an onion whole with the skin on. This protective layer helps seal in the nutrients. Simply drizzle with oil, seasoning and optional balsamic vinegar before baking at 200°C/400°F/gas mark 6 for roughly one hour. Remove the skin before eating.

Go raw: Chop raw red onion through a salad to make the most of its active nutritional benefits.

⬚ Skin

Onion skins are edible, and because they contain everything the plant needs to protect itself, the skins are very rich in flavonoids such as

quercetin, which can be anti-inflammatory. The skins can be boiled into broths or ground and added to dishes.

Veggie offcuts broth: Add the skins and root end to a veggie offcuts broth (see pages 232–4 for my recipe).

Onion powder: Add one teaspoon of ground onion skin to bread dough. This can be ground in a mortar and pestle, but for larger amounts use a blender. Whilst the taste is very subtle, it gives an antioxidant boost to your baking. Or try adding this to batter for dishes like battered onion rings, fried tofu or savoury pancakes. Try my onion skin-infused focaccia with caramelized red onions recipe (below). Onion powder is best used fresh but can also be saved in a jar for around a week.

Ramp-up your rice: To give rice an added nutritional boost, steep the whole skins in the water whilst the rice cooks and remove before serving.

Compleat Recipe: Onion Skin-Infused Focaccia with Caramelized Red Onions

The addition of ground onion skin to this bread gives a very subtle flavour and a huge antioxidant boost. Collect your onion skin peelings (the papery outer shell) in the freezer until you are ready to use them. You can also incorporate the skin from garlic bulbs. Use as little or as much as you have saved, up to four tablespoons. The finished bread is alive with colour from the onions. You could also try topping with fresh rosemary, olives or sun-dried tomatoes.

Prep 30 minutes, plus proving.
Cooking 20 minutes **Makes** 1 loaf

• Skin from about 5 medium-sized onions (any type will work)
• 300g/10½oz strong white bread flour
• 7g/¼oz (or 1 sachet) fast-action dried yeast
• 1 teaspoon salt
• 135ml/4.5fl oz/½ cup extra-virgin olive oil, plus extra for oiling and to serve
• 1 medium red onion, sliced
• Sea salt flakes, for sprinkling

1 In a blender, blitz the onion skins to fine flakes. Set aside.

2 Combine the flour, yeast, salt and three tablespoons of the olive oil in a large bowl. Mix in the onion flakes. Slowly add 175ml/6fl oz/scant ¾ cup water and mix to a sticky dough.

3 Knead for roughly 6 minutes until it forms a soft and stretchy dough. Lightly oil the dough ball and leave in the bowl, covered with a tea towel. Let prove for 1 hour, or until doubled in size.

4 Oil an 18cm/7in square baking tin. Punch down the dough before kneading briefly and tipping into the baking tin, pressing the dough so that it fills the space. Leave to rise for 30 minutes.

5 In a frying pan, sauté the red onion with three tablespoons water until soft and caramelized. Set aside until the dough is ready. Preheat the oven to 220°C/425°F/gas mark 7.

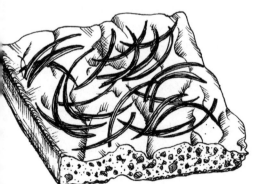

6 Once risen, make dimples in the dough using your fingers. Drizzle over the remaining olive oil, top with the onions and sprinkle with sea salt flakes. Bake for 20 minutes until a golden colour. Serve warm with extra olive oil over the top or for dipping if desired.

▦ Green-fingered ideas

Natural plant care: Scattering onion and garlic skins around the base of any plants or vegetables you are growing acts as a natural deterrent for slugs and snails.

Regrown onion offcuts: Experiment with planting the offcut root end of an onion. Using a 2cm/¾in-deep piece, rest it in a saucer with a little water, using cocktail sticks to stand it upright if needed. Place on your windowsill for up to a week, until the roots begin to grow. Change the water regularly and be careful not to let it get mouldy. If roots and growth appear, plant it in a pot with moist soil so that the roots are buried and the top exposed. Keep in a sunny spot and water regularly. The roots will continue to grow, and the onion top will sprout new growth. This sprout will taste spring onion/scallion-like and can be chopped and eaten before allowing to grow back again. Planting offcuts is often a case of trial and error, but if you're lucky then your plant will eventually create a flower, from which you can collect onion seeds to replant again!

♲ Household projects and ideas

Onion skins natural fabric dye: Onion skins contain everything you need to create a natural dye with beautiful earthy tones. Place the skins in a large pan of water and bring to the boil. Let this simmer for up to one hour or until you are happy with the colour of the water. The more skins you use, the more intense the colour, and adding red onion skins will give a deeper hue.

Turn off the heat, then allow to cool a little before straining out the skins and composting them. You can use this liquid to fully colour fabrics, but it's fun to experiment with a natural tie dye. Natural fabrics will work best. Scrunch your fabric or clothing into the desired tie dye pattern and fix with elastic bands. Carefully submerge your piece in the onion skin water, ensuring it is fully covered. Leave it to absorb the dye for eight hours, then unwrap and rinse under cold running water. Leave to hang dry and you're done!

You can use this same technique with other natural dyes – like turmeric, tea leaves, beetroot peel, berries, avocado stones (pages 22–3) and coffee grounds – however, onion skins are especially magical because they contain the natural chemicals needed to fix and seal the dye, even when washed.

⊠ Spring onion/scallion

The white and green parts of spring onions are edible and tasty, and even the roots can be eaten (they're surprisingly full of flavour!) Chop whole spring onions through salads and over curries, ramen or stir fry. Also try sautéing the green, leafier part or grilling/broiling whole. Spring onions/scallions are best stored in the fridge in a glass with a little water, root end down. If you grow your own spring onions or have an abundance of them, they can be chopped and frozen ready to add to dishes. You can also try regrowing from an offcut 2cm/¾in root piece of spring onion. Follow the same steps as you would for an onion root (page 172).

Parsnip

Earthy but sweet, parsnips are a must in a plant-based roast dinner. They can also be eaten raw, thinly shredded in a salad. Try them boiled and mashed or add to stews and soups. There's usually no need to peel this root vegetable,

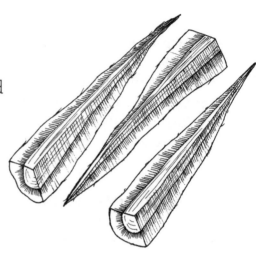

and any offcuts can be used to make a homemade stock.

IN SEASON: September – March

MAKE IT LAST! Parsnips are best stored in the fridge.

NUTRITIONAL BENEFITS: Parsnips are a great source of folate, vitamin C and fibre. Like many vegetables, much of the parsnip's nutrients are found in and close to the skin.

Parsnips were named as part of the "dirty dozen" in recent research. This means that unfortunately they are high on the list of produce with multiple pesticide residues, so it's especially worth buying organic if you can and washing your parsnips well.

EDIBLE AND USEFUL PARTS: Flesh, core and skin.

▣▣ Flesh and core

For years, I removed the core from my roasted parsnips, believing it was too tough and woody. However, once roasted or boiled the core is just as tasty and useful as the whole parsnip. Enjoy your whole parsnips roasted, boiled and mashed with butter or blended into soups.

▣ Skin

Save yourself a job and leave the skin on your parsnips. The skin stores much of the nutrients so compleating means you're making the most of this root vegetable. If you do peel your parsnips, save the peels to make crisps.

Peel crisps: Peel the skins, toss them in a little oil and season with salt and pepper. Bake evenly on a tray at 180°C/350°F/gas mark 4 for eight to ten minutes to create tasty crisps. For more about veggie peel crisps, see pages 214-5.

▣ Odds and ends

Offcuts broth: Along with other vegetable scraps, freeze the hard parsnip top in a tub and save to make stock (see my recipe on page 232). You could also include the peels.

Kimchi: Parsnip ends and offcuts, as well as the whole sliced parsnip, are great as a more unusual addition to fermented kimchi. Find my recipe on pages 133–5.

☑ My favourite ways to compleat:

Roasted skin-on parsnips: Step away from the peeler! Save yourself time and leave the skin on your parsnips when roasting. Slice the parsnips lengthways, leaving the core attached. If the core is especially large, make sure it is divided between pieces. Roast in an ovenproof dish with a little rapeseed/canola oil and seasoning, such as salt, pepper and fresh rosemary, at 190°C/375°F/gas mark 5 for around 40 minutes.

Spiced parsnip soup: Dice one onion and sauté in ½ tablespoon rapeseed/canola oil in a large saucepan. After a few minutes, add two diced garlic cloves and one teaspoon cumin seeds. Chop five parsnips, including the core and skin, into cubes and add after another minute. (The parsnip ends can be saved for making stock at a later date, along with the onion and garlic peels. Recipe on page 232.) Add one teaspoon curry powder and ½ teaspoon ground turmeric. Stir and after one minute, pour in 700ml/24fl oz/3 cups stock. Stock can be shop bought or homemade. Season with salt and pepper, and if using homemade stock, be generous with the salt. Simmer over a medium heat with the lid on for around 25 minutes, until the parsnips are soft. Add 400ml/14fl oz/1¾ cups plant milk and ¼ teaspoon ground cinnamon. Blend with a hand blender until smooth. Serve warm, topped with optional chilli flakes, toasted seeds and chopped fresh coriander/cilantro leaves and stalks.

Root vegetable gratin: You can leave the skin on when making a creamy baked root vegetable gratin. For my celeriac gratin recipe, see pages 77–8, and swap the celeriac for vegetables like parsnips or potatoes.

Compleat Recipe: Cheezy Whole Parsnip Dip

When creating this recipe, I had a hunch that parsnip would make a brilliant plant-based cheeze substitute. I was inspired by a recipe on Gena Hamshaw's blog *The Full Helping* and gave it a compleating twist, using the parsnip's core, peel and flesh. This dip is delicious on crackers or with tortilla chips. To make more of a meal of it, dollop it onto squares of puff pastry along with your choice of veggies, such as fresh tomatoes, and bake. You could even use it to stuff pasta, like cannelloni or tortellini.

Prep 10 minutes **Cooking** 10 minutes
Makes enough for 4 to share as a dip

- 4 medium parsnips
- 8 tablespoons nutritional yeast

- 2 tablespoons miso paste
- 2 teaspoons olive oil
- ½ teaspoon garlic powder
- ½ teaspoon smoked paprika
- Salt and black pepper

1   Chop the parsnips into even pieces, leaving the skins on and including the core. Remove just the very hard ends and save those to make broth at a later date if you wish (pages 232–4). Boil the chopped parsnip in a saucepan of lightly salted water for around 10 minutes until soft.

2   Strain the parsnips and leave them to cool a little before adding them to a food processor with the nutritional yeast, miso paste, olive oil, garlic powder and smoked paprika. Blend for a few minutes until smooth. Taste and season with salt and pepper. Decant into a jar and allow to cool before storing in the fridge for up to a week. Simple but delicious.

Pastry

Don't let offcut pieces of pastry go to waste as they are still tasty and useful for making mini desserts or savoury treats.

MAKE IT LAST! Pastry should be stored in the fridge. Any offcuts can be rolled into a ball and tightly wrapped in reusable food wrap to store in the fridge for a couple of days or the freezer for a few months. Defrost before using.

♻ How to revive old pastry

If old pastry has dried out but is still safe to eat, splash it with a few drops of water and microwave it for a few seconds. This brings the pastry back to life and makes it much more moist and easier to work with.

▦ Uses for pastry offcuts

Pie for one: Try filling a small pie dish with chopped vegetables and fresh herbs, like sage and rosemary and optional grated plant-based cheeze.

Season it with salt and pepper and pour in enough stock to cover. Top with the pastry and bake according to the pastry's instructions.

Mini tarts: Cut leftover pastry into circles and press each round into a greased cupcake baking tray. Top with jam or pesto before baking according to the pastry's instructions for an easy sweet or savoury tart.

Pastry straws: Roll or twist your leftover pastry into sticks and sprinkle over a little salt, plant-based cheeze and/or nutritional yeast. Alternatively, try yeast extract for a more unusual flavour. Line a baking tray with baking paper and spread the straws out evenly. Bake at 190°C/375°F/gas mark 5 for 10–15 minutes until cooked.

Pineapple

Historically, pineapples were seen as a status symbol – a sign of adventure with their striking skin and crown. Today, we usually throw much of the pineapple away when we eat it. However, the skin does have various uses, and the core is edible and healthy. Designers even make leather alternatives from the fibres of pineapple leaves.

IN SEASON: Pineapples are at their best in spring and summer. It's worth considering the carbon footprint of tropical fruits like this.

MAKE IT LAST! Store pineapples at room temperature and eat as soon as possible once ripe. To check, pluck a leaf – it should come away easily. When preparing, twist off the leafy crown, rather than slicing, to reduce wastage.

NUTRITIONAL BENEFITS: Pineapples contain vitamins A and C and are the only source of the enzyme bromelain, which is found in the flesh and even more so in the core. Bromelain has been found to help reduce inflammation and boost immunity. The tougher core also contains extra fibre.

EDIBLE AND USEFUL PARTS: Flesh, skin and core.

⌧ Flesh

Pineapples' sweet flesh is delicious raw and in smoothies, juices and desserts. If your pineapple has gone slightly overripe, don't discard it as this can be perfect for slicing into a pineapple upside-down cake. Any harder or unused offcuts can be frozen to add to drinks. These can also be fed sparingly in small pieces as a treat for dogs. My dog Bella loves a few small pieces chilled on a hot day.

Dried pineapple slices: Drying is great way to preserve fruit. Cut the pineapple into slices, as thinly as possible, including the core. Spread evenly on a baking tray and cook at 100°C/200°F/gas mark ¼ for two to three hours, until fully dried. Eat as a snack or topping for smoothie bowls, granola (pages 238-9) and desserts. Follow this same process with different fruits, like apricots and kiwi, and ideally bake one big batch of dried fruits at once. Store in a jar for up to a month.

⌧ Skin

Whilst eating pineapple skin isn't much fun, you can simmer the cleaned skin to create a distinctive broth or drinks like tepache or tea.

Fermented pineapple tepache: This traditional Mexican recipe uses the skin and core of one pineapple to create a refreshing, gut-friendly drink, perfect with ice on a hot day or a splash of rum or gin. Wash your pineapple before peeling and coring and save the flesh for another dish. In a large saucepan, bring 3l/105fl oz/13 cups water to the boil. Remove from the heat and dissolve 250g/9oz/1¼ cups sugar (brown or raw cane). Add the pineapple skin, chopped core and one stick of cinnamon. Cover the saucepan with a dish towel to allow air but stop debris. Leave at room temperature out of direct sunlight for two days or up to a week, to taste and depending on conditions. Froth on the surface is a good sign and means it is fermenting. Once ready, taste – you can add more sugar or dilute with water as desired.

It should taste sweet but pleasantly funky. Strain out the core and skin, and compost. Pour the liquid into bottles and store in the fridge for up to a month.

▣ Core:

The core of a pineapple is where most of the bromelain is stored. Blend it into smoothies, juices or piña colada. The core can be chopped and frozen to save and use later.

Pineapple core salsa: Turn to pages 149–50 for my duo of fruit salsas, including pineapple core pico de gallo.

Pineapple core syrup: Chop and weigh your pineapple core and place in a jar with the same weight of caster/superfine sugar and some optional citrus peels (lime works well). Muddle well and seal the jar. Leave this overnight and you will wake up to a sweet liquid. If the sugar has not quite dissolved, muddle a little more, add a small splash of water and leave for a few more hours. When ready, strain through a fine-mesh sieve/strainer, squeezing as much juice out of the fruit as possible. Store in a jar in the fridge for up to a month and add to drinks. The used core and peels can be composted.

Chop into curries: Pineapple core adds a nice dash of sweetness to a curry. Try chopping it into chunks and adding to the sauce at the same time as vegetables like potatoes and carrots. It works well in a sweet and sour, and also complements a coconut-based curry.

Pineapple Core Fritters with Cinnamon Sugar

Turn a leftover pineapple core into a compleat treat with this easy fritter recipe. It's sweet and delicious – great served with plant-based vanilla ice cream and cinnamon sugar. I like to roast the pineapple core before making the fritters as cooking softens it and makes it easy to prepare.

Prep 5 minutes. **Cooking** 45 minutes
Serves 2

- 1 pineapple core (reserve the flesh for another dish)
- Coconut oil, for brushing
- 1 teaspoon baking powder
- 60g/2½oz/scant ½ cup plain/all-purpose flour
- 1 tablespoon caster/superfine sugar
- ¼ teaspoon ground cinnamon
- Rapeseed/canola oil, for cooking
- Plant-based vanilla ice cream, to serve

1 Place the whole pineapple core in an ovenproof dish and brush with a little coconut oil to prevent it from drying out. Bake in the oven at 180°C/350°F/gas mark 4 for 25–30 minutes, until softened. Remove from the oven and, once cooled a little, chop the core into even slices and set aside.

2 To make the batter, sift the flour and baking powder into a bowl and whisk in 100ml/3½fl oz/scant ½ cup cold water. Set aside for 10 minutes. In a small bowl, make the cinnamon sugar by mixing the sugar with the cinnamon.

3 Once the batter has rested, heat the oil in a frying pan over a medium to high heat. Start with one tablespoon of oil and add more as you go if the pan dries out too much. Test that the oil is hot enough by dropping a pinch of flour into the pan. It should sizzle.

4 Using tongs, dunk each piece of pineapple core into the batter mix, ensuring that it is well coated, and then place in the frying pan. Fry until golden and crispy – this should take around 1 minute per side. If needed, drizzle a little extra batter on top of each slice once it is in the pan.

5 Once cooked, remove from the heat. Serve warm in bowls with a generous dusting of cinnamon sugar and a scoop of plant-based ice cream.

♻ Household projects and ideas

Save a handful of pineapple skin with as little flesh attached as possible. Place in a tub on your car's dashboard. As the peelings dry out, they will release a sweet aroma, creating a natural air freshener. Compost after a couple of weeks. Also try this with citrus peelings.

Potato

Potatoes are a staple in every kitchen but don't overlook their peels – that's where most of the taste and nutrients are stored. My potato recipes provide little twists on traditional dishes, to help reduce waste of this favourite root vegetable.

IN SEASON: April – July

MAKE IT LAST! Keep potatoes in cool dark place, loose or in a cloth or paper bag or sack. Stored properly, they can last for months. I store mine in a strong paper sack in the shed.

NUTRITIONAL BENEFITS: Potatoes are a source of vitamins B6 and C, as well as potassium, fibre and iron. Much of the nutritional content is stored in the skin, which is a source of protein and fibre. Research has found the skins to be especially rich in calcium, magnesium, potassium, iron and zinc.[1]

EDIBLE AND USEFUL PARTS: Flesh and skin.

1 Nijolė Vaitkevičienė, "A comparative study on proximate and mineral composition of coloured potato peel and flesh". *Journal of the Science of Food and Agriculture*, 2019.

Flesh

I very rarely peel potatoes, but there are some dishes where just the flesh might be preferable, such as roasted potatoes.

Roasted potatoes: Roast dinner is my favourite meal to cook. I've experimented with skin-on roasties but peeling the potatoes comes up trumps for giving them a fluffy texture. Next time you're cooking a roast, save the peelings to make yourself some peel crisps to enjoy whilst you wait for everything else to cook. A win-win!

⚑ Peel

There's often no need to peel your potatoes. If you do, there's lots of ways to make use of the skins. Also experiment with leaving the skin on in dishes like curries, mash, roasties and potato salad – it adds a nice subtle texture.

Peel crisps: Peel the skins, toss them in a little oil and season with salt and pepper. A little garlic powder is also a tasty addition. Spread evenly on a tray and bake at 180°C/350°F/gas mark 4 for eight to ten minutes to create tasty crisps. For more about veggie peel crisps, see page 214-5.

Veggie offcuts broth: Add any unused potato skins or offcuts to a veggie offcuts broth (see pages 232–4 for my recipe). Or why not boil and blitz them into a leek and potato soup?

Potato Peel Cheezy Scones

The starch in potato peels helps create bread that is light and moist. You can collect your potato peelings in an airtight container for a couple of days in preparation. If you don't have quite enough peelings, then simply add as many as are available.

Prep 15 minutes. **Cooking** 25 minutes
Makes roughly 12 scones

- 100g/3½oz potato peelings
- Plant butter, for greasing and serving
- 1 teaspoon white wine vinegar
- 225ml/8fl oz/scant 1 cup soya or almond milk

- 300g/10½oz self-raising flour, plus extra for dusting
- ½ teaspoon baking powder
- 3 tablespoons nutritional yeast
- ½ teaspoon chives (fresh or dried)
- ¼ teaspoon garlic powder
- 3 tablespoons olive oil
- 1 teaspoon Dijon mustard
- ¼ teaspoon salt

1   Blanch the potato peelings in a saucepan of boiling water and let simmer for 5 minutes until the peels are softened a little. Strain and leave to cool.

2   Preheat the oven to 220°C/425°F/gas mark 7 and grease a baking tray with a little plant butter. In a jug, mix the white wine vinegar into the milk and set aside.

3   In a bowl, mix the flour, baking powder, nutritional yeast, chives and garlic powder. Set to one side.

4   In a food processor, blitz the cooled potato peelings until they form small chunks. Add the peelings to the bowl with the dry ingredients. Add the olive oil, mustard, milk and vinegar mix and season with the salt. Combine to form a dough. If too wet or sticky, add a little more flour. If too dry, add a little extra milk.

5   Tip the dough onto a floured surface and knead briefly then roll out to a thickness of 2.5cm/1in. Use a cutter or glass to cut the dough into 5cm/2in circles, reworking any offcuts. Place, spaced apart, on the prepared baking tray. Bake in the oven for 10–12 minutes until lightly golden. Serve warm, spread with plant butter.

☑ My favourite ways to compleat:

Baked whole or Hasselback: Enjoy a traditional jacket potato – best baked in the oven for around one hour to create delicious, crispy outer skin and fluffy flesh. Also try Hasselback potatoes by making deep scores into the uncooked potatoes every few millimetres with a knife. Place in a baking tray, season with salt and pepper and drizzle with a little oil. Bake at 200°C/400°F/gas mark 6 for an hour or until soft inside.

Skin-on potato wedges: Chop the potatoes into wedges, leaving the skin on. Heat a frying pan with rapeseed/canola oil 1cm/½in deep. Once hot, use tongs to place the potatoes in the oil and cook, turning regularly, for 15–20 minutes. Remove from the pan and place on a sheet of paper towel to absorb any excess oil. Serve with salt and vinegar.

Root vegetable gratin: You can leave the skin on potatoes when making a creamy baked gratin. Follow my celeriac gratin recipe (pages 77–8) and swap the celeriac for potatoes or a mixture of root veggies.

Potato salad: New potatoes are perfect for a skin-on potato salad, but there's no reason why you can't use any potatoes. Boil them in a saucepan for 10–15 minutes before allowing to cool. Mix with plant-based mayonnaise (make your own with aquafaba on page 87), chopped spring onions/scallions, chives and seasoning to taste.

Compleat colcannon: Traditionally made with mashed potato, greens and cream, I like to mash my potatoes with a generous glug of plant milk and a dollop of plant butter. Simmer and mash the potatoes with the skin on. To make the greens, in a frying pan, sauté one to two cloves of chopped garlic in one teaspoon of plant butter and add your choice of greens - chopped cauliflower leaves are delicious. Cook for a few minutes, then fold through the mashed potatoes.

Green-fingered ideas

If you've ever left potatoes in the cupboard for too long then they may have started sprouting (also known as chitting). You can remove these eyes and eat the potatoes as normal (as long as the potatoes haven't turned green – these can be harmful). You could also try planting them! I have successfully grown potatoes from old potatoes that were sitting at the bottom of a sack, wrinkly and covered in eyes. Plant in spring for potatoes in summer. Choose sprouted potatoes of around 5 x 5cm/ 2 x 2in. If your potatoes are large, cut them into pieces this size, ensuring each piece has at least one sprout. Dig a trench in your garden, 12cm/5in deep, and place one potato piece every 30cm/12in. Cover with earth, water and allow to grow and harvest as you would with shop-bought seed potatoes. These can also be grown in a large container. Plentiful food for free with no waste!

Sweet potato

Sweet potatoes are rich in fibre and vitamins A, B6 and C. They were named as part of the "clean 15" in recent research. This means that they were found to contain little, if any, pesticide residues! Sweet potatoes can be used skin-on in the same way as white potatoes. I especially love a simple sweet potato jacket filled with salad and seeds, skin-on sweet potato fries and adding chunks of skin-on sweet potato to a dahl with red lentils and spinach.

Pumpkin

If you think pumpkins are just for carving, then think again! In my home, we spend the day cooking pumpkin soup, curry and pie, as well as peel crisps, toasted seeds and oaty pumpkin dog treats for Bella. Just one pumpkin can go so far; they are full of flavour and there are many creative ways to use them in your kitchen. If you do carve and light your pumpkin, consider salvaging it after Halloween and donating it to your local animal rescue sanctuary to help feed residents, such as pigs.

IN SEASON: September – December

MAKE IT LAST! Pumpkins can be harvested and stored for months – making it even more of a shame that we only celebrate them for a short period each year. Store them whole and in a cool, dry place. If you'd rather, chop or purée the flesh and freeze it, ready to add to dishes.

NUTRITIONAL BENEFITS: Pumpkin flesh and skin are rich in potassium and vitamin A. They contain calcium and magnesium, and also provide vitamins C, E and some B vitamins. The seeds are also packed with nutrients, including protein, omega-3 and omega-6 fatty acids, iron, calcium, folate and vitamins A and B2.

EDIBLE AND USEFUL PARTS: Flesh, skin and seeds.

▣ Flesh

Pumpkin flesh is full of flavour and is so versatile that it can be used in both sweet and savoury dishes. The skin is tender enough to be left on for many recipes. Try pumpkin flesh boiled or roasted in curries, desserts and soups, such as my squash soup recipe on pages 206–8. Pumpkin can also be roasted and mashed to use as you would a butternut squash to make a flavoursome pasta sauce (page 204).

Autumn spice-roasted pumpkin: Try roasting a pumpkin whole. Remove the seeds, drizzle with a little rapeseed/canola oil and sprinkle over one to two teaspoons of ground mixed spice. Bake in an ovenproof dish at 190°C/375°F/gas mark 5 for 40 minutes to two hours (depending on the size of your pumpkin). Delicious served with a mix of grains, such as bulgur wheat with brown lentils. This also works well with different varieties, such as the Crown Prince squash.

Spiced seeded pumpkin muffins: These muffins are topped with pumpkin seeds and filled with warming spices. Peel and cube 300g/10½oz of pumpkin. Simmer in boiling water for 15–20 minutes, until soft enough to blend to a purée. Strain and leave to cool before blending. Once puréed, add to a bowl with 100g/3½oz/½ cup granulated sugar,

100ml/3½fl oz/scant ½ cup rapeseed/canola oil and one teaspoon vanilla extract. Sift in 200g/7oz/1½ cups plain/all-purpose flour, two tablespoons baking powder, one teaspoon ground cinnamon, ½ teaspoon ground ginger and ¼ teaspoon ground nutmeg. Add 40g/1½oz chopped pecans and combine using a spoon, being careful not to over mix. Grease a muffin tray and spoon in the mixture evenly, filling each hole half to three-quarters full, so that you have 12 muffins. Bake for 20–25 minutes in the oven at 180°C/350°F/gas mark 4 until cooked through and a golden orange colour. Allow to cool in the tray. For an optional topping, toast the pumpkin seeds on a baking tray for eight to ten minutes whilst the muffins are cooking. Once the muffins are cooked and cooled, brush them with a little maple syrup and sprinkle over the toasted seeds.

Hearty Pumpkin Curry

This warming coconut curry is especially tasty because the skin is left on the pumpkin. If you can't get hold of a pumpkin then use a squash of your choice – a Crown Prince, butternut or kabocha squash would work well. Serve with rice or bread and sprinkle over chopped fresh coriander/cilantro.

Prep 20 minutes. **Cooking** 1 hour
Serves 4

- 1 medium pumpkin – around 1kg/2lb 4oz
- 1 teaspoon coconut oil
- 1 medium white onion, diced
- 1 medium courgette/zucchini, sliced
- 3 medium garlic cloves, finely chopped
- ½ red chilli, plus optional seeds
- 5cm/2in piece of root ginger
- 1 teaspoon cumin seeds
- 2 teaspoons medium curry powder
- ½ teaspoon ground turmeric
- Small bunch of fresh coriander/cilantro
- 400ml/14fl oz/1¾ cups coconut milk (canned or make your own, recipe on pages 107–8)

- 200ml/7fl oz/scant 1 cup stock
- 2 handfuls of fresh spinach (100g/3½oz)
- Salt
- Rice or bread, to serve

1   It can take some time to prepare the pumpkin so do this first. I use one medium pumpkin, cubed and with the skin on – around 1kg/2lb 4oz worth. You can also include any of the stringy guts from inside the pumpkin. Toast the seeds to eat as a snack whilst the curry is cooking or save them for another dish.

2   Heat the coconut oil in a large saucepan. Add the onion and cook for a few minutes over a low to medium heat, then add the courgette. Cook for 5 minutes whilst dicing the garlic cloves and chilli. (Save the onion and garlic skins for making broth if you wish, page 232-4.) I include the chilli seeds too, but leave those out if you don't want much heat. Add the garlic and chilli to the pan and grate in the root ginger, including the skin.

3   After a further 1 minute, add the cumin seeds and mix well. Wait a few minutes for the seeds to crackle a little and smell aromatic. Add the prepared pumpkin, curry powder, ground turmeric and the chopped stalks from the coriander. Save the coriander leaves to sprinkle over the top when serving.

4   Stir and add the coconut milk and stock. Bring to the boil, then cover with a lid and allow to simmer for 45 minutes or until the pumpkin has softened. Add the fresh spinach and allow it to wilt into the curry for a couple of minutes.

5   Stir and season with salt to taste, being generous if you have used homemade stock. Remove from the heat and serve with rice or bread. Chop the remaining fresh coriander over the dish.

⊡ Skin

Peeling a pumpkin is not the easiest of tasks, so for dishes like soup and curry, leave the skin on – it adds flavour and is a good source of fibre. If you do remove the peel, save it to make natural, packaging-free crisps.

Sweet or savoury pumpkin peel crisps: Peel the skins, toss them in a little oil and season with salt and pepper. Spread evenly on a tray and bake at 180°C/350°F/gas mark 4 for eight to ten minutes to create tasty crisps. Try different savoury flavours by adding chilli powder, smoked paprika or garlic powder before cooking. Or for sweet crisps – great for serving with pumpkin pie or as a snack – use a little oil and sprinkle the peels in sugar and cinnamon before cooking.

⊡ Seeds

Pumpkin seeds are full of useful goodness, like protein, fibre and iron. We often buy them pre-prepared from a shop, so why not harvest your own from your pumpkin? Sprinkle them over salads and soups or add to homemade bread, crackers and granola. If your pumpkin is especially large, then the seeds may be too big and crunchy. However, you could instead save these to plant and grow your own pumpkins.

Toasted pumpkin seeds: Separate, rinse and dry the seeds, then toast on a baking tray in the oven at 180°C/350°F/gas mark 4 for 10-15 minutes. Great for adding to salads, granola and homemade cereal bars or energy balls. Also try mixing the seeds in a little oil, salt and spices before cooking. Smoked paprika or chilli powder work well or try ground cinnamon for a sweeter taste.

Seed butter: Just like nuts, seeds can be made into butter. Toast the seeds (as above) and blend in a food processor, adding a little salt and oil of your choice as you go. Be patient and watch the magic happen. For my no-waste nut and seed butter recipes, go to page 237.

Seed pesto: Use the toasted seeds in place of nuts to make a flavoursome, nut-free vegan pesto. See pages 67 and 158 for my recipes and use whatever greens you have available – carrot tops, beet leaves or spinach are great substitutes for traditional basil.

▦ Odds and ends

Offcuts broth: Along with other vegetable scraps, freeze the hard parts of the very end of the pumpkin in a tub, plus any leftover peelings, and save to make stock (see my recipe on page 232-4).

Compleat Recipe: Pumpkin Pie, Served with Caramelized Seeds

This sweet pie is filled with delicious pumpkin and autumnal flavours. Serve it with optional caramelized pumpkin seeds and sweet pumpkin peel crisps (page 193). Make your own pastry by following the recipe below, or use a shop-bought shortcrust pastry.

Prep 40 minutes, plus chilling time
Cooking 1 hour 10 minutes
Serves 8

For the pastry:
- 300g/10½oz/2¼ cups plain/all-purpose flour
- 25g/1oz/3 tablespoons caster/superfine sugar
- 150g/5oz/2/3 cup chilled plant butter
- Pinch of salt

For the filling:
- 1 medium pumpkin, weighing around 1kg/2lb 4oz
- 400ml/14fl oz/1¾ cups coconut milk (canned or make your own, recipe on pages 107–8)

- 2 tablespoons maple syrup
- 1 teaspoon vanilla extract
- 1½ teaspoons ground cinnamon
- ½ teaspoon ground ginger
- ¼ teaspoon ground nutmeg
- ¼ teaspoon salt

For the caramelized seeds:
- Seeds saved from the pumpkin
- 1 teaspoon rapeseed/canola oil
- 1 tablespoon plant butter
- 1 tablespoon caster/superfine sugar
- 1 teaspoon ground cinnamon

1 First, make the pastry by using your hands to combine all of the pastry ingredients in a bowl, rubbing together with your fingertips to make a crumbly consistency. Add two tablespoons water and work to form a ball of dough. Leave to chill in the fridge for at least 10 minutes, or overnight if you wish.

2 Roll out the pastry to 5mm/¼in thick and use it to line a round 25cm/10in shallow pie dish. Prick the base of the pastry with a fork a few times. This needs to be blind baked so cover the pastry with baking paper and fill with baking beans. If you don't have these, you can substitute with dried beans or rice (but you won't be able to eat them afterwards so save them to reuse as baking beans). Bake in the oven at 180°C/350°F/gas mark 4 for 15–20 minutes until the pastry is firm and golden.

3 Meanwhile, prepare the pumpkin. Remove and save the skin and seeds. Cube the flesh into even pieces and simmer in a saucepan of boiled water for 20 minutes until soft enough to purée. Strain and allow to cool before using.

4 In a food processor, blend the pumpkin to a purée and add the coconut milk, maple syrup, vanilla extract, cinnamon, ginger, nutmeg and salt. Mix well, ensuring it is all combined. Pour into the prepared pie crust and bake at 180°C/350°F/gas mark 4 for 45–50 minutes until cooked and firmed. Allow to cool, then set further in the fridge for at least 2 hours before serving.

5 Sweet pumpkin peel crisps and caramelized seeds are optional toppings to really make the most of your pumpkin. For the sweet peel crisps recipe, see page 193, and prepare these fresh just before serving. To make the caramelised seeds, rinse the seeds well and shake off as much excess water as possible. Toast them by coating them in the rapeseed oil, spreading them evenly on a baking tray and cooking in the oven at 180°C/350°F/gas mark 4 for 10–15 minutes. To caramelize, heat the butter in a frying pan and add the toasted seeds and sugar. Mix well and cook for a few minutes. Remove from the heat and tip the seeds into a bowl with the cinnamon. Mix well and add more sugar or cinnamon if needed. Serve sprinkled over the pie with sweet peel crisps also, if you wish.

▣ Green pet foods

Pumpkin, oat and turmeric dog treats: My dog, Bella, is such a huge part of my life; but since getting older she's had a number of health issues. I'm therefore really careful what I feed her and try to stick to a natural diet, giving her food as much care as I would my own. She loves vegetable treats, like steamed pumpkin, broccoli and carrot. However, these baked treats are great to really spoil her. I've included optional turmeric, which is thought to be anti-inflammatory and boost immunity. You'll need 250g/9oz of pumpkin flesh, peeled or unpeeled (whatever you prefer). Boil it for 20 minutes until soft then strain and leave it to cool. Once cooled, purée the pumpkin in a food processor with 170g/6oz/1 2/3 cups rolled oats, one tablespoon coconut oil, one teaspoon milled chia seeds, one teaspoon milled flax seeds and half to one teaspoon ground turmeric (depending on your dog's size and taste). Once well blended, a dough should form. Remove it from the processor, roll into a ball and leave to rest for ten minutes. Once rested, use a rolling pin on a lightly floured surface to roll the dough to a thickness of around 5mm/¼in. Using a cookie cutter, cut the dough into treat shapes and place on a non-stick baking tray. Bake in the oven at 180°C/350°F/gas mark 4 for 15–20 minutes until firm. Allow to cool before giving them to your dog. Feed as a treat and store in an airtight jar for up to a week.

▦ Green-fingered ideas

You can save pumpkin seeds to plant and grow from. To do this, rinse the seeds under cold running water to remove as much of the flesh and guts as possible. Spread the seeds out on a plate or an absorbent layer (like a paper towel) to soak up the moisture and leave them in a warm cupboard for a few weeks until completely dry. You can then store them in an envelope ready to sow in spring.

Radish

With their beautiful array of colours, radishes may be small but they are packed with a distinctive peppery flavour. The whole plant can be eaten, from root to leaf top. Enjoy radishes raw in salads, slaws or summer rolls. They are also great for adding some flavour and crunch to a stir-fry; or try roasting them and serving with sautéed radish leaves

IN SEASON: May – October

MAKE IT LAST! Radishes are best stored in the fridge. If you grow your own or have an abundance, try pickling or fermenting them.

NUTRITIONAL BENEFITS: Radishes are a great source of folate and potassium, as well as vitamins B2, B6 and C. They also contain some calcium, iron and magnesium. The radish leaves are especially nutritious and are filled with antioxidants, fibre and the same goodness as the radish bulb with even more vitamin C.

EDIBLE AND USEFUL PARTS: Flesh, skin and seeds.

▣ Flesh

The whole radish root can be eaten. There's no need to peel or trim each one. It's all full of goodness and flavour. Try them in a salad, roasted or pickled.

Pickled radishes: Crunchy and peppery, radishes are great sliced and pickled. This is also a good way to preserve a harvest of radishes. Turn to page 235 for my easy pickling recipe. These work well pickled with some sliced root ginger and fresh chilli.

Summer rolls: These look impressive but are very easy to make. Slice raw vegetables like radish, cucumber, carrot, spring onion/scallion and broccoli stalk into strips and wrap them in rehydrated rice paper to create little parcels. You could also include some of the radish leaves or serve my radish, carrot and ginger salad on the side (page 199). Summer rolls are great with sweet chilli or peanut sauce for dipping.

Kimchi: Radishes are great sliced and fermented in a kimchi to give it an extra spicy hit. Turn to pages 133–5 for my kimchi recipe.

✐ Leaves

Radishes are part of the mustard family and the leaves share a similarly peppery taste, although it is more subtle than that of the radish bulb. Use them raw or cooked, as you would other greens, adding them to soups, stews and curries. Also try them sliced raw through a salad, sautéed with olive oil, salt and garlic or blended into homemade hummus (pages 84–5) to add extra colour and goodness.

Mixed greens pesto: Radish leaves can be used in place of traditional basil in pesto. Find my pesto recipe on page 158. You can use a mixture of greens to create a unique flavour, such as carrot tops, beet leaves, radish leaves or spinach.

☑ My favourite ways to compleat:

Roasted radishes: We tend to think of eating radishes raw, but they are also great roasted. Slice each radish in half and reserve the leafy tops.

Toss the radish bulbs in a little rapeseed/canola or olive oil and roast at 180°C/350°F/gas mark 4 for around 20 minutes, until softened and roasted. Serve as is or add to a pan with the shredded leaves, a little oil and a squeeze of lemon juice. Sauté briefly over a medium heat to wilt the leaves and combine. Taste and season with sea salt.

Compleat Recipe: Citrusy Whole Radish, Carrot and Ginger Salad

This raw salad makes the most of a fresh bunch of radishes, incorporating both the roots and leaves. The dressing has lemon and sesame flavours, which work well with the peppery radish roots.

Prep 10 minutes, plus resting time

Serves 2 as a main or 4 as a side

- 10 radishes, with tops
- 1 carrot

- 1cm/½in piece of fresh root ginger
- 1 tablespoon lemon juice
- 1 teaspoon sesame oil
- ½ teaspoon rice vinegar (optional)
- 2 teaspoons sesame seeds

1 Finely shred the radishes and their leaves – no need to trim them, everything can be added. Place them in a bowl and grate in the carrot, including the skin. Then grate in the root ginger, with the skin included too. If there's any stringy parts of the ginger, mince those with a knife and add them.

2 Pour over the lemon juice, sesame oil and rice vinegar. Mix well and scatter in the sesame seeds. Mix again and leave to rest for 10 minutes. Serve chilled.

⊞ Green-fingered ideas

If you've ever grown radishes and left one of the plants to go to seed, then you know that they produce seed pods. These are edible and are becoming a popular delicacy. When picked young, they can be enjoyed whole. They have a faintly peppery, spicy taste. You could also save a few of the seeds from these pods to dry and then sow to grow more radishes.

Spinach (and other greens)

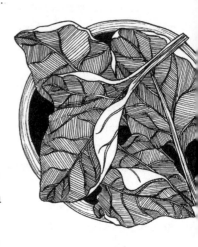

I love spinach raw because you can really appreciate the taste and texture – great as a side, in salads and as a nutritious alternative to lettuce in sandwiches and wraps. It's also tasty sautéed or added to curries, stews and dahl. If you have lots to use up, try blending spinach into pesto (which can be enjoyed fresh or frozen in portions), adding it to a smoothie or transforming it into pasta dough. Most spinach recipes can be adapted to other greens you might have an abundance of, such as chard, kale or spring greens. These are also a good way to use up other more unusual greens, like turnip and beet tops or cauliflower leaves.

IN SEASON: Year-round, but best from March to September.

MAKE IT LAST! Spinach is best stored in the fridge. You can also freeze spinach to add to curries, stews and soups.

NUTRITIONAL BENEFITS: Spinach is an excellent source of iron, folate, manganese, protein and vitamins A, C and K.

EDIBLE AND USEFUL PARTS: Leaves and stalks.

☑ My favourite ways to compleat:

Stir into dahl or curries: This is a great way to use up spinach that may be wilted or less tasty raw. You can make a quick dahl by sautéing chopped red onion and garlic with grated root ginger. Add two handfuls of dry red lentils, 375ml/13fl oz/1½ cups water, two teaspoons curry powder and ½ teaspoon ground turmeric. Season and simmer for 20 minutes. One minute before removing from the heat, stir through generous amounts of spinach.

Sag aloo: Heat two tablespoons coconut oil in a pan and sauté one chopped onion, two diced garlic cloves and a grated 2.5cm/1in piece of unpeeled root ginger. Add 500g/1lb 2oz chopped potatoes (skin on) and stir in one teaspoon cumin seeds, one teaspoon chilli flakes, ½ teaspoon ground turmeric and one teaspoon curry powder. Season well. After five minutes add a splash of water. Cover and simmer for ten minutes. Stir through 250g/9oz spinach and one teaspoon nigella seeds. Serve!

Vegan huevos rancheros: Spinach is a great addition to plant-based breakfasts. This Mexican-inspired brunch is one of my favourite recipes (see page 95-7) - the tofu is poached in a spiced tomato sauce with peppers and spinach, served with coriander/cilantro and avocado.

Compleat Recipe: Garden Greens Pici Pasta

Traditional "pici" pasta is easy and enjoyable to make by hand at home. The method originates from Tuscany and I like to add any greens I have in the kitchen or need to use up. I remember when I first tasted pici pasta at a vegan café in Kent and couldn't believe the dough only used flour and vegetables! This version includes spinach and fresh green beans, but the recipe is quite flexible.

You can replace or supplement the spinach with greens like chard and turnip or beet tops, or add in a handful of fresh basil or wild garlic leaves.

Prep 30 minutes. **Cooking** 5 minutes. **Serves** 4

For the pasta:
- 200g/7oz fresh spinach
- 100g/3½oz green beans, chopped
- 320g/11¼oz/2¼ cups plain/ all-purpose flour, plus extra for dusting
- Salt

For the dressing:
- 4 cloves garlic, peeled and sliced
- 60g/2½oz pine nuts, or chopped nuts of your choice
- 10 sundried tomatoes (or use homemade semi-dried tomatoes, page 223)
- 4 tablespoons olive oil
- Chilli flakes (optional), to serve

1 In a food processor, combine the spinach, green beans, flour and a pinch of salt. Blend until a dough is formed – this shouldn't be too wet. Remove the dough from the food processor and separate into two portions. Roll each portion on a lightly floured worktop until each makes a long piece of around 1m/40in in length. Use the side of a spoon to cut into pieces, every 1–2cm/ ½–¾in. These should resemble little green sausages.

2 Bring a large pan of salted water to the boil and carefully drop the pasta pieces into the water. Simmer for around 5 minutes until the pasta floats to the top. Don't overcrowd the pan and cook in batches if needed.

3 At the same time, sauté the garlic, pine nuts and sundried tomatoes in the oil for a few minutes. When ready, strain the pasta and toss it in the dressing. Serve warm with an optional sprinkling of chilli flakes.

🪴 Green-fingered ideas

Try growing perpetual spinach. This is easy to grow from seed and, once ready, can be harvested down to the base of each stalk. The leaves will quickly grow back, giving you a supply of fresh spinach for months. If you don't have space outdoors, perpetual spinach can be sown in medium-sized pots on decking, a windowsill, or in a window box.

Squash (butternut)

It was squash and pumpkins that first sparked my imagination about compleating. They are delicious and versatile – even more so when you make full use of their bounty. The flesh, skin and seeds are all edible and delicious. If, like me, you always have a squash in your kitchen then you'll never lack for meal inspiration. Choose butternut squash for a nutty, creamy taste, and experiment with the different varieties available, such as the chestnut-tasting kabocha, delicious orange hubbard and nifty spaghetti squash.

IN SEASON: September – December

MAKE IT LAST! Squash is one of the longest lasting vegetables. It will keep for months if stored in a cool, dry place. If you'd rather, chop the flesh and freeze to later make soups, curries or stew.

NUTRITIONAL BENEFITS: All squash are a great source of fibre, vitamins and minerals. The butternut squash is rich in vitamins A, B6 and C – great for supporting your immunity and eye health. The seeds are a brilliant plant-based source of protein, and the skin is just as nutritious as the flesh.

EDIBLE AND USEFUL PARTS: Flesh, skin and seeds.

⬚ Flesh

Delicious in just about anything! Roast,
boil, mash or blend. Particularly good
in curries, soups, salads or mixed with
quinoa and herbs.

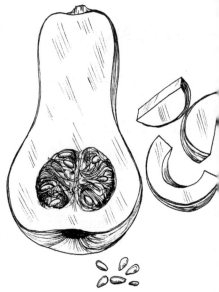

Butternut pasta sauce: This is one of
my favourite comforting dishes, and it's
so simple to make. Roast the chopped
flesh of a medium-sized butternut
squash at 190°C/375°F/gas mark 5 in one
tablespoon of olive oil with two cloves
of garlic. Season with salt and pepper
and one teaspoon of dried rosemary
or a fresh sprig. Once soft, mash well to create a creamy pasta sauce. For
a cheesier taste, add one tablespoon of nutritional yeast. Serve stirred
through pasta. A dash of chilli oil is optional! Also try my roasted butternut
squash ravioli recipe on pages 88–90.

⬚ Skin

There's often no need to remove the skin of the softer varieties of
squash, like the butternut. Chop and cook the squash with the skin
on, and it can be cooked in the same way as you would normally use
the flesh. If you do peel the skin, roast it for a natural, packaging-free
alternative to crisps.

Peel crisps: Peel the skins, toss them in a little oil and season with salt
and pepper. Spread evenly on a tray and bake at 180°C/350°F/gas mark
4 for eight to ten minutes to create tasty crisps. These are really
flavoursome as is, but you could also try adding chilli flakes, smoked
paprika or garlic powder.

⊞ Seeds

Rich in fibre and protein, cooked butternut seeds have a nutty flavour and make a healthy snack. Some squash seeds are larger and harder, so you might prefer to cook and blitz these into a dish (such as a pesto) rather than enjoying whole.

Toasted seeds: Separate, rinse and toast the seeds on a baking tray in the oven at 180°C/350°F/gas mark 4 for ten minutes to then add to salads, granola and homemade cereal bars. Or try mixing the seeds in a little oil, salt and spices before cooking; smoked paprika works especially well. I love using these as a topping for soups, avocado toast or as a snack.

Seed butter: Just like nuts, seeds can be made into butter. Toast the seeds (as above) and blend in a food processor, adding a little salt and oil of your choice as you go. Be patient and watch the magic happen. (For my no-waste nut and seed butter recipe, see page 237.)

Seed pesto: Use the toasted seeds in place of nuts to make a flavoursome vegan pesto. See pages 67 and 158 for my recipes and use whatever greens you have available - carrot tops and beet leaves are great substitutes for traditional basil.

▦ Odds and ends

Offcuts broth: Along with other vegetable scraps, freeze the hard parts of the very end of the squash in a tub and save to make stock (see my recipe on pages 232-4).

☑ My favourite ways to compleat:

Whole stuffed squash: Slice in half, remove the seeds and bake at 200°C/400°F/gas mark 6 with the skin on for roughly one hour until soft.

Stuff with your favourite grains and veg, such as quinoa and fresh parsley or mint. Pomegranate seeds add a nice twist. Delicious served with salad, toasted seeds and a drizzle of plant-based plain yogurt.

Compleat Recipe: Spiced Butternut Squash Soup Topped with Toasted Seeds and Crispy Skins

This soup is warming, delicious and waste-free. Swap the butternut squash for any squash or pumpkin you have available. However, butternut and orange hubbard squash are especially great for giving the dish extra creaminess. If you have any greens that need using up (kale or cauliflower leaves work well), throw those in after you blend the soup.

Pushed for time? Leave the squash in chunks, rather than blending; or you could try with the skin on the squash and follow the same steps. Or double the ingredients and freeze half to save time another day.

Your stock can be shop-bought or made from vegetable offcuts. Start collecting things like carrot ends, offcut veg and onion peel in a tub in the freezer. Once you have enough, create your own veggie offcuts broth (recipe on pages 232–4).

The toasted seeds will keep for two weeks in an airtight jar. Experiment with any spices you like. Crispy skins are best eaten fresh.

Prep 25 minutes
Cooking 45 minutes
Serves 4

- 1 medium butternut squash (or squash of your choice)
- 3 garlic cloves
- Rapeseed/canola oil, for roasting
- ½ teaspoon smoked paprika
- 1 teaspoon coconut oil
- 1 white onion, diced
- 2.5cm/1in piece of fresh root ginger, skin on, grated
- ¼ teaspoon cumin seeds
- 400ml/14fl oz/1¾ cups coconut milk (canned or make your own, recipe on pages 107–8)
- 240ml/9fl oz/1 cup vegetable stock (see pages 232–4 for my veggie offcuts broth recipe)

- ¼ teaspoon dried chilli flakes
- ½ teaspoon curry powder
- Any leftover greens you need to use up (optional)
- Salt and black pepper
- Handful of fresh coriander/cilantro (use the full stalks and leaves), to serve

1   Preheat the oven to 180°C/350°F/gas mark 4. Peel and chop the squash into small chunks. Save the ends if you want to make stock at a later date. Separate the peel and seeds into two bowls.

2   Put the flesh in an ovenproof dish with the garlic cloves and a glug of rapeseed oil. Roast for 35–40 minutes until soft, mixing halfway through cooking.

3   Meanwhile, toss the squash peel in ½ teaspoon of rapeseed oil and a sprinkle of salt. Lay out evenly on a baking tray and pop in the oven for 8–10 minutes until crispy, turning halfway through cooking.

4   Rinse the seeds in a fine-mesh sieve/strainer to remove any pulp. Shake dry and toss in a bowl with ½ teaspoon of rapeseed oil, a sprinkle of salt and the smoked paprika. Mix until coated. Spread out evenly on a baking tray and cook for 10 minutes, mixing halfway through cooking.

5   Set the cooked seeds and skins aside and turn the oven off once the flesh is finished.

6   In a large saucepan, heat the coconut oil. Add the onion and cook for 1 minute before adding the root ginger. Stir well and cook for 2 more minutes. Add the cumin seeds and cook for around 30 seconds until they smell aromatic and crackle a little. Throw in the roasted squash and garlic, stir and cook for 1 further minute.

7   Add the coconut milk and stock and stir. Simmer for 2 minutes before turning

off the heat and blitzing with a hand blender. Stir well, checking that the garlic has blended.

8   Return the pan to a medium heat and add the dried chilli flakes and curry powder. Add any chopped greens you wish to use up and simmer until tender. Season with salt and pepper as desired. Heat until warm and well mixed.

9   To serve, chop over the fresh coriander leaves and stalks. Top with the toasted seeds and crispy skins.

▦ Green-fingered ideas

You can save squash seeds to plant and grow from. To do this, rinse the seeds under cold running water to remove as much of the flesh and guts as possible. Spread the seeds out on a plate or an absorbent layer (like a paper towel) to soak up the moisture and leave them in a warm cupboard for a few weeks until completely dry. You can then store them in an envelope to sow in spring.

Strawberries

When in season, strawberries are delightfully sweet and full of flavour – perfect for compleating an entire punnet's worth. Strawberries are not technically a fruit though, but a member of the rose family, and both the leaves and the berries are edible.

IN SEASON: May – September

MAKE IT LAST! Strawberries are best stored in the fridge. If you have strawberries that will soon go off, chop and freeze them for blending into smoothies.

NUTRITIONAL BENEFITS: Strawberries are a great source of vitamins C and K, as well as fibre, folate, manganese and potassium. They also contain significant amounts of phytonutrients and flavonoids. Both the strawberry and the leaves are full of antioxidants.

EDIBLE AND USEFUL PARTS: Flesh, seeds, core and leaves.

⌨ Berry

Serve fresh and whole with the leafy tops attached – and there's definitely no need to core your strawberries. Try using strawberries as a more unusual choice in a crumble, or as a topping for a sweet and warming French cinnamon toast brunch (pages 40–2).

Dried strawberries: Cut your strawberries into thin slices or quarters. Spread evenly on a baking tray and cook at 100°C/200°F/gas mark ½ for two to three hours, until fully dried. Eat as a snack or topping for smoothie bowls, granola and desserts. Follow this same process with different fruits, such as apricots and kiwis, and ideally bake one big batch of dried fruits at once. Store in a jar for up to a month.

Strawberry coulis: This is a great way to use up any strawberries or other berries. You'll need roughly six parts strawberries to one-part icing/confectioner's sugar and a splash of lemon juice (substitute that for water if you need to). So, for 300g/10½oz strawberries, add 50g/1¾oz/heaped 1/3 cup icing sugar. Chop the strawberries and simmer them over a medium heat with the icing sugar and a splash of lemon juice for five to ten minutes until broken and a sauce is forming. Serve with desserts as a slightly chunky strawberry sauce or purée using a hand blender.

🍃 Leaves

The green leafy crown on top of a strawberry is called a calyx and is edible. Eat whole with the berry or, when preparing your strawberries, twist the leafy top off to carefully separate the two. I recommend cutting off the little stalk, if attached, as it can be rather twig like! The leaves are fragrant but not overly sweet, so can be eaten raw, chopped through a salad or used to top a dish, like strawberry pancakes (pages 211–12). You could also blend the leaves into a strawberry smoothie, to give it an added green boost, or add them as decoration in drinks such as cocktails or homemade lemonade (page 101).

Strawberry tops tea: With their subtly sweet taste, the leaves from the top of strawberries are great for making herbal tea. Steep a handful of the leaves in boiling water for up to five minutes before straining and drinking warm. Also try cooling the liquid and serving chilled as iced tea or steeping with a few fresh mint leaves for a mint and strawberry leaf infusion.

☑ My favourite ways to compleat:

Strawberry-infused spirits: Strawberries and their leaves can be used to infuse spirits. Find my simple recipe on pages 235–6 and experiment with combinations like strawberry and mint gin or berry-infused vodka.

Balsamic baked strawberries: This uses whole strawberries, as well as the leaves, with very few other ingredients to easily make a really rich dessert. It works well with fresh strawberries but is also a good way to use up any which are past their best. Slice the strawberries from a 250g/9oz punnet in half, leaving the leafy tops attached. Place them in a bowl with two tablespoons balsamic vinegar and one tablespoon caster/superfine sugar. Mix well and leave to marinade for ten minutes. Transfer the strawberries and liquid to an ovenproof dish and bake at 190°C/375°F/gas mark 5 for 20–30 minutes until the strawberries are softened and caramelizing. Serve hot with plant-based ice cream or yogurt. Drizzle over any of the remaining balsamic liquid from the dish.

Compleat Recipe: Strawberry Pancakes, Topped with Strawberry Leaves

My girlfriend makes the most amazing American-style pancakes and, given the option, I'll request a stack of them for breakfast every day. It makes my mouth water just writing about them! We like to incorporate different toppings, like chopped nuts, bananas, blueberries or strawberries. And the best thing is that they work especially well with fruit that's slightly overripe, so by eating these pancakes you're doing your bit to avoid food waste! I like to top mine with strawberry leaves, which complement the sweetness of the pancakes.

Prep 10 minutes **Cooking** 20 minutes
Makes 2 generous stacks (about
6–8 pancakes)

- 120g/4¼oz/1 cup buckwheat flour
- ½ teaspoon baking powder
- 1 tablespoon caster/superfine sugar
- Pinch of salt

- 200ml/7fl oz/scant 1 cup plant milk
- 1 teaspoon vanilla extract
- 2 teaspoons apple cider vinegar
- 200g/7oz strawberries, including leaves
- 2 teaspoons rapeseed/canola oil
- Plain plant-based yogurt, to serve
- Golden/light corn syrup, to serve

1   In a bowl, combine the flour, baking powder, sugar and salt. Use a hand whisk to make sure they are well mixed. Add the plant milk, vanilla extract and apple cider vinegar and mix gently to combine.

2   Slice the strawberries into quarters. Twist off the leaves and reserve to scatter over the finished pancakes. Any hard stalks should be composted.

3   Warm a small frying pan over a medium to low heat. Pour the oil into a ramekin so that you can easily use a little per pancake. You don't want them to be too greasy.

4   Using a baking brush, brush the base of the heated pan with a thin layer of the oil. After 30 seconds, ladle 60ml/2fl oz/¼ cup of the pancake mix into the pan. This should spread to form a lovely round pancake. Into this, scatter 6–10 pieces of the chopped strawberries. The pancake should start to bubble and fluff up quickly. Once the edges begin to set, flip the pancake. Check it regularly and cook for a few minutes until both sides are lightly browned. The consistency should be soft, fluffy and cooked through. When ready, remove from the pan and set aside on a plate.

5   Repeat this process for each of the pancakes, until you have two stacks of three to four pancakes. Serve the stacks with a dollop of yogurt. Drizzle over the golden syrup and scatter over the strawberry leaves. Enjoy warm.

Swede/rutabaga

We tend to just think of swede/
rutabaga as peeled and mashed,
but there's lots more you can do
with this often-unappreciated
vegetable. Swede is thought to
have originated as a result of a
cross between a turnip and wild
cabbage. It's especially tasty
roasted with the skin on and can be added to pies, pasties,
gratin and even curry, or grated raw into a salad or slaw.

IN SEASON: October –
February

MAKE IT LAST! Swede can be
stored at room temperature
for a few days but is best kept
in the fridge if you don't plan
to use it quickly. Swede can
also be pickled or fermented
to preserve it for longer.

NUTRITIONAL BENEFITS:
Swede is really high in vitamin
C and is also a source of
calcium, potassium and
vitamin B6. It is also a good
source of fibre, particularly in
the skin.

Swede was named as part
of the "clean 15" in recent
research. This means that they
were found to contain little, if
any, pesticide residues!

EDIBLE AND USEFUL PARTS:
Flesh, skin and leaves.

⬚ Flesh

Sweet and earthy, swede is commonly mashed with butter and pepper, but can also be roasted as a side or chips, blended into soups and added to stews, pies, pasties and more.

⬚ Skin

There's often no need to peel your swede, but if you do then save the peelings to make natural, packaging-free crisps (recipe follows).

No Fuss, No Waste Vegetable Peel Crisps

These are one of the most satisfying ways to reduce waste in your kitchen. I often prepare a bowl of vegetable peel crisps, ready to munch on or share with guests whilst the rest of the meal cooks. Even those who are dubious about cooking with "scraps" are converts once they try vegetable peel crisps! You can use the peelings from any root vegetables, such as potatoes, sweet potatoes, parsnips, carrots, beetroots, turnips and celeriac/celery root, as well as pumpkin, squash and swede peelings.

Prep 5 minutes **Cooking** 10 minutes

- Vegetable peelings
- Rapeseed/canola oil, to coat
- Salt and black pepper
- Dips, to serve

Suggested extra seasoning:
- **Spicy:** Smoked paprika and/or chilli powder. Also great with some garlic salt.
- **Earthy:** Garlic powder and fresh or dried rosemary.
- **Curried:** Ground cumin and/or curry powder.

Different oils to try:
- Chilli oil
- Garlic oil
- Sesame oil
- Homemade herb-infused oil

1   Wash your vegetables before peeling then save the peels in a bowl. Use the peelings from just one vegetable variety or a mixture. Make sure they are dry, then add enough oil to lightly coat, but not smother, them. You could use rapeseed oil or add a splash of one of the suggested flavoured oils to create a more powerful taste.

2   Season the peels with salt and pepper. There's no need to add extra seasoning if you want the natural flavour of the vegetablesto reallyshine through. However, if you wish, try adding any of the suggested extras - some good combinations are curried parsnip peels, spicy pumpkin peels or herby beetroot peels.

3   Mix the peels well to ensure that they are well coated. Spread evenly on a baking tray and cook in the oven at 180°C/350°F/gas mark 4 for 8–10 minutes until crispy. Check regularly and mix halfway through cooking to make sure that the peels don't burn.

4   Enjoy your crisps warm or cooled. They are best eaten fresh. Serve with optional dips, such as harissa (page 95) or garlic mayonnaise (page 87) or homemade hummus (pages 84–5).

🌿 Leaves

Unfortunately it is rare to ever find swedes sold in shops with their leafy tops complete. However, if you grow your own or manage to source them, swede tops are edible, much like beet or turnip leaves. Use them as an alternative to cabbage and other greens. They are great added to a soup or stew, or try them sautéed in plant butter and garlic.

☑ My favourite ways to compleat:

Maple roasted swede and sprouts with nuts: Swede is delicious unpeeled and roasted in chunks as an alternative addition to roast dinner. Also try it roasted with a little maple syrup, sprouts and walnuts for a subtly sweet, delicious side. See the brussel sprout chapter for the recipe, page 57.

Root vegetable gratin: Add unpeeled, sliced swede to a creamy baked gratin. For my celeriac gratin recipe, see pages 77–8, and swap the celeriac for swede or other skin-on root vegetables.

Fermented swede: Shredded unpeeled swede can be used as an alternative to cabbage to ferment into a slightly sweet, tasty take on a sauerkraut (page 62). Or add fine slices of unpeeled swede along with other vegetables to make a spicy fermented kimchi (pages 133–5). Kimchi commonly uses turnips, but swede works just as well.

Skin-on swede wedges: Chop the swede into chip wedges, leaving the skin on. Toss in rapeseed/canola oil and season with salt and pepper. Add your choice of flavouring, such as ground cumin, mixed herbs or garlic powder. Roast in the oven for 45 minutes to one hour and enjoy as an alternative to potato chips.

🍲 Odds and ends

Offcuts broth: Along with other vegetable scraps, freeze any hard parts of your swede, plus any leftover peels, and save to make stock (see my recipe on pages 232–4).

Tea leaves & coffee grounds

Don't let your spent coffee grounds or leftover tea leaves and bags go to waste. They can be useful in the kitchen or garden. I like to store mine in an airtight container in the fridge for a few days until I'm ready to use them.

♻ Choosing plastic-free:

Many tea bags may look innocent, but they are often made using plastic. This unfortunately means that they can't be composted and can leech microplastics. Where possible, choose certified plastic-free tea bags or loose-leaf tea, which are safe to compost. Teabags like these tend to be more expensive but also have a much stronger flavour. I like to use each teabag twice – once in the morning and again for my afternoon cuppa. Compostable and plastic-free coffee packs and pods are also available.

📓 Homemade teas

Try making your own teas from fresh or dried homegrown herbs and flowers, such as mint, lemon balm, lavender or chamomile. You can also create teas from offcuts, like apple peel (page 11), fresh lemon and root ginger (page 132), strawberry tops (pages 210–11), orange peel (pages 99–100) and fennel fronds (pages 123–4).

♲ Baking with spent coffee grounds

Spent coffee grounds still retain some flavour so can be used as a coffee substitute in recipes like cookies, chocolate cakes and sauces. To make coffee-infused cream, try adding one-part coffee grounds to two parts plant-based cream and leaving for a few hours in the fridge before straining through a muslin cloth/cheesecloth to remove the grounds. Whip with a whisk and it is perfect for topping cakes or tiramisu.

♲ Wellbeing uses

Coffee grounds face and body scrub: To make a natural scrub, save coffee grounds in the fridge and mix one-part coffee grounds with one-part brown sugar and one-part coconut oil. Stir well and store in a jar in the fridge for up to a week. This is naturally exfoliating and moisturising. You could also add a little citrus juice, vanilla extract or essential oil.

▦ Green-fingered ideas

Coffee grounds are rich in nitrogen, which is great for the garden or house plants. I scatter spent grounds around plants, dig them into the soil or add them to my compost heap. They naturally decompose and give the earth and plants some added nutrients.

They are also said to help deter ants, slugs and the like from sensitive crops, like lettuces. Used tea leaves can also be beneficial in the garden, compost heap or for house plants. If using a tea bag, cut the leaves free from the bag and empty them onto the soil. They contain some nitrogen and will naturally break down.

Tofu

Whether scrambled, baked, battered or added to dishes like stir-fry, ramen and Thai curries, tofu is incredibly versatile and absorbs flavours well. Made from soybeans, tofu is high in protein, calcium and iron. If you plan to scramble your tofu, then there's no need to press it in advance. However, for most other dishes, pressed firm tofu will achieve a better texture.

♻ Environmental considerations

You may have heard that soya milk and products have been criticized for contributing to deforestation. Although it does have an impact, it's worth noting that according to The Vegan Society, only 6 per cent of global soya produced is consumed by humans, the remaining 94 per cent is used in animal feed.

Make it last! Most firm tofu should be stored in the fridge, whilst silken tofu can normally be stored at room temperature (check the packet). Once opened, any leftover tofu will last for two days stored in an airtight container in the fridge – you could add a little water to help the tofu maintain its freshness. A block of firm tofu can also be stored in the freezer. This not only helps preserve the tofu but also reduces excess moisture, so that it better absorbs any marinades or sauce. The tofu should be drained and pressed before freezing and placed in a freezer-safe container. Use within five months and allow the tofu to thaw before cooking. It's great for crispy marinaded tofu.

Press ahead

Pressing tofu improves its texture in many dishes. I like to use a simple tofu press, left in the fridge for a few hours or overnight, before cooking dishes such as stir fry, curry, vegan huevos rancheros or ramen. You can make a DIY tofu press by sandwiching your tofu block between sheets of kitchen roll on a large plate. Place something heavy, like a few tin cans, on top to act as a weight and leave for a few hours so that the tofu presses and releases its liquid.

Nutritional benefits: Tofu is a great source of protein and also contains essential amino acids, iron, calcium and other minerals.

My favourite ways to cook tofu:

· **Tofu scramble with carrot lox and asparagus:** my veg royale brunch. Recipe on pages 16–17.

· **Poached tofu in a spicy tomato sauce with peppers and courgette, served with coriander and avocado:** my vegan huevos rancheros. Recipe on pages 95–7.

· **Crispy fried tofu:** try my ramen recipe on pages 53–5, served with sesame tofu, mushrooms and broccoli. To make your tofu extra crispy, coat it in a layer of cornflour/cornstarch before frying and ensure the pan is very hot.

Tomatoes

Over summer, tomatoes are at their most flavoursome.
If you grow your own, try drying or roasting them to
preserve your harvest into the colder months. Not sure
what to do with a heap of green tomatoes that won't ripen?
These can be fermented or cooked into a chutney – perfect
with crackers or as a gift. For a more unusual salad, try
adding fresh tomatoes to my tabbouleh recipe (pages
68–9) or bake and incorporate them into a vegan huevos
rancheros brunch (pages 95–7).

IN SEASON: June – October
but at their best in August.

MAKE IT LAST! Tomatoes
continue to ripen after
picking so unless they are
beautifully ripe, store on
a countertop to enhance
their flavour and maturity.
However, once very ripe,
tomatoes go bad so eat
them as soon as possible
or store them in the fridge.
My recipes for semi-dried
tomatoes and roasted
tomato sauce are ideal for
an abundance of tomatoes.

NUTRITIONAL BENEFITS:
An excellent source of
vitamin C, beneficial
for immunity and iron
absorption, and vitamin A,
essential for growth, vision
and reproduction.

EDIBLE AND USEFUL PARTS:
Flesh, seeds and vine.

🌱Vine

Although the tomato vine and leaves aren't edible, the vine can be used to infuse a roasted tomato sauce or passata. Add the vine to the pan with your tomatoes and simmer for a few minutes to add a subtle taste – great if your tomatoes are out of season and less flavoursome. Remove the vine before serving. Tomatoes are also delicious roasted on the vine, drizzled with a little olive oil and sprinkled with salt and pepper (compost the vine after cooking).

☑ My favourite ways to compleat:

Oven roasted chopped tomato sauce: If, like me, you grow tomatoes, then a homemade sauce is a must. This also works just as well with ripe shop-bought tomatoes. Use this recipe as a flavour-filled alternative to canned chopped tomatoes for stirring through pasta, topping pizza and adding to dishes. In a baking dish, place 500g/1lb 2oz fresh tomatoes, two halved garlic cloves and one chopped shallot or small red onion. Add any herbs to taste, such as a handful of fresh basil, oregano, rosemary or a few chilli flakes, as well as a little salt and pepper. Pour over one tablespoon olive oil and ½ teaspoon balsamic vinegar. Roast at 170°C/325°F/gas mark 3 for 45 minutes to one hour, depending on size, until the tomatoes break down and release juices. Use as desired. This can be served chunky or blitzed using a hand blender. Serve fresh, store in the fridge for a few days or freeze.

Semi-dried tomatoes: These are sweet and full of flavour, great for adding to dishes. If you grow your own tomatoes, this is a good way to preserve a large batch. These can be made in a dehydrator or dried in an oven on the lowest temperature, around 60°C/140°F/gas mark ¼, for around five hours. Cut your tomatoes into pieces the size of half a cherry tomato and spread them evenly on a baking tray. Cook until dried. Once cooled, pack into a jar with olive oil and optional flavourings, such as a few sliced garlic cloves, fresh herbs like oregano and basil, or dried mixed herbs. Store in the fridge and eat within a few weeks. Use the infused oil from the jar for cooking or drizzling over dishes.

Bruschetta: Put your tomatoes centre-stage on a bruschetta. Lightly grill/ broil thick slices of baguette or your choice of bread. Once toasted, rub each slice generously with a garlic clove to infuse the flavour. Top with chopped fresh tomatoes, torn basil, a drizzle of olive oil and salt and pepper to taste.

Ratatouille: Made with fresh tomatoes, courgette/zucchini and aubergine/ eggplant, homemade ratatouille is so delicious. Turn to page 117 for my recipe.

Salsa: You can't beat homemade salsa. For my slightly less traditional takes on this spicy dip, try my kiwi salsa verde recipe on pages 149–50 and sweetcorn relish recipe on page 111.

Compleat Recipe: Plant-Based Spaghetti Puttanesca

This is a favourite in our house and is rich in flavour from the fresh tomatoes, parsley and olives. It's also a great dish to make use of the flavoursome brine from jars of olives and capers. If you have them to hand, also try substituting the parsley with chopped carrot tops. This recipe uses fresh tomatoes, but a can will also do the job. Great served with focaccia (page 129) or garlic bread.

Prep 5 mins. **Cooking** 15 mins
Serves 4

- 1kg/2lb 4oz fresh tomatoes (ideally plum), chopped into small cubes or two 400g/14oz cans chopped tomatoes
- 1 tablespoon rapeseed/canola oil
- 3 garlic cloves, minced
- 20 kalamata olives, pitted and chopped
- Small red chilli, diced (plus seeds if you wish)
- 4 tablespoons capers
- Large handful fresh parsley, roughly chopped
- 500g/1lb 1oz pack dried spaghetti
- 4 tablespoons tomato purée/paste
- 2 tablespoons olive brine (from the kalamata olives jar)
- 2 tablespoons caper brine (from the capers jar)

1   Cook the fresh tomatoes over a medium heat in a pan for 10 minutes. Allow to reduce down and release their liquids to create a chunky sauce.

2   In a large pan, heat the oil over a medium heat. Add the garlic, olives, capers and chilli. I like to include the chilli seeds, but only include these if you like the spice. Separate the stalks from the parsley and chop and add these to the pan. Stir and allow to cook for 2–3 minutes.

3   Meanwhile, cook the spaghetti according to the packet's instructions – simmering for roughly 10 minutes in a pan of boiling water. Pour your chopped tomato sauce (or the cans of chopped tomatoes if not using fresh) into the other pan, along with the tomato purée, olive brine and caper brine. Allow to simmer on a low to medium heat, stirring occasionally.

4   When the spaghetti is ready, drain and add it to the sauce. Mix well and chop through the remaining parsley. Serve with bread and (optional) red wine.

🏡 Green-fingered ideas

Tomatoes are so rewarding and delicious when homegrown. They are also perfect for a balcony or windowsill if you don't have much outside space. You can even use a tomato to grow from during the spring months, rather than buying a packet of seeds. To do this, slice the fresh tomato into a few even slices, bury it 2.5cm/1in deep in a container with compost and water well. If your tomato is large, slice off and eat the flesh, burying just the seeded part. Place on a windowsill, keep moist, and sprouts will start to appear after one to two weeks. Once big enough, repot and grow these as you would shop-bought seeds or plants.

Use up green tomatoes: If you grow tomatoes then it can be a common problem that some do not ripen, especially toward the end of the season. Contrary to common belief, tomatoes can ripen without lots of sunlight, as long as they are kept warm. Once it is too cold outside, collect your green tomatoes and bring them inside. Place them, with space for airflow between each fruit, on a plate or alternatively in a paper bag or cardboard box. Leave a ripe banana with your tomatoes (you can make banana bread from it afterwards!) and the ethylene from the banana will help naturally ripen your tomatoes. Check on your tomatoes regularly over a couple of weeks. This technique works best with tomatoes that have started to turn from green to yellow but can also be used with green tomatoes. Green tomatoes are also delicious cooked into a chutney or fermented for a few days with sliced onion and crushed coriander seeds.

Green Tomato and Apple Chutney

Rather than letting any homegrown green tomatoes go to waste, you can make a tasty tomato and apple chutney. This recipe was passed down to me from my stepmum's mum and is a favourite. Great as a gift or on crackers with vegan cheeze.

Prep 15 minutes **Cooking** 45 minutes
Makes three 500ml jars

- 450g/16oz green tomatoes
- 170g/6oz apples
- 170g/6oz onions
- 85g/3oz sultanas/golden raisins
- 85g/3oz sugar of choice
- 140ml/4½fl oz/generous ½ cup vinegar of choice
- 1 teaspoon ground ginger
- 1 heaped teaspoon salt

- 1 tablespoon pickling spice (shop bought or homemade)

To make your own pickling spice (makes 1 small jar):
- 2 tablespoons mustard seeds
- 2 teaspoons coriander seeds
- 1 teaspoon ground ginger
- 1 teaspoon chilli flakes
- 1 bay leaf, crumbled
- 5cm/2in piece of cinnamon stick, crumbled
- ¼ teaspoon ground cinnamon
- ¼ teaspoon ground nutmeg

1 To make the pickling spice, combine all the ingredients in a small jar.

2 For the chutney, chop the tomatoes, apples and onions into even chunks. Save the onion skins to make stock (page 232) and the apple peels and cores to make apple cider vinegar (pages 12–13) at a later date if you wish, or compost them.

3 Combine all of the ingredients except the spice in a large saucepan. To add the pickling spice, tie it in a small piece of muslin cloth/cheesecloth and add to the pan. Simmer uncovered for 45 minutes to allow the chutney to reduce, stirring and checking every 10 minutes. Decant while hot into sterilized jars (page 232). Store unopened for up to 6 months and store in the fridge once open.

Turnip

In Roman times, turnips were used as ammunition to catapult disapprovingly at unpopular public figures. In Charles Dickens's novels, if you called someone a "turnip", you meant that they were a moron. And during wartime Britain's food shortages, turnips were one of few choices, making them rather unpopular – all doing nothing to boost their reputation to this day. Nonetheless, I love turnips! They are delicious fermented, pickled or roasted and can be eaten from root to leaf top, so go on, give turnips a chance.

IN SEASON: June and July for sweeter baby turnips, and through to February for stronger tasting winter turnips.

MAKE IT LAST! Turnips are best stored in the fridge and can last for months. Separating the roots from their leafy tops helps the turnip roots to stay fresh for longer, so it's best to eat the greens quickly.

NUTRITIONAL BENEFITS: Turnip greens are really nutritious and are beginning to be sold separately as a "superfood" in some shops. They are a great source of calcium, folate and vitamins C, E and K. The turnip root is also a good source of fibre, vitamins and minerals, especially vitamin C.

Turnips were named as part of the "clean 15" in recent research. This means that they were found to contain little, if any, pesticide residues!

EDIBLE AND USEFUL PARTS:
Flesh, skin and leaves/tops.

⌷ Flesh

Crunchy and slightly spicy when raw, turnips are perfect for fermented dishes, whilst their taste is sweeter and earthy when cooked. You can enjoy turnips without peeling the skin. Try them roasted, mashed, fermented or shredded raw through a salad or slaw with carrots.

Kimchi: One of my favourite ways to eat turnips is fermented. Kimchi is a spicy ferment which is delicious with slices of turnips, carrots and cabbage. Turn to pages 133–5 for the recipe.

Fermented Turnip Pickles

In our house, these are called unicorn carrots after we heard at a vegan market about a child who had spotted the bright pink turnip batons on a stall and excitedly declared that they must be the carrots of unicorns! Fermented or pickled turnips are popular in Middle Eastern cuisine and get their bright colour from a few slices of beetroot. They are delicious with falafels and salad in a wrap or pitta bread, and because these are fermented, they are great for boosting your gut and overall health. It's important to ensure everything is clean when fermenting, so wash your produce and hands well and use clean utensils when checking the taste of the turnips.

Prep 10 minutes, plus fermenting time **Makes** one 750ml jar

- 250g/9oz turnips
- 1 small raw beetroot
- 2 bay leaves (optional)
- 2 garlic cloves, peeled (optional)
- 1 tablespoon fine sea salt
- 500ml/17fl oz/2 cups beet water (page 35, optional) or water

1   Chop the turnips and beetroot into thin wedges, leaving the skin on. Place these into your sterilized jar, leaving as few air gaps as possible. It is usually easiest to pack the jar if you insert the vegetables in consecutive circles, rather than just chucking them in. Tuck the optional bay leaves and garlic cloves into any gaps.

2   In a jug, dissolve the sea salt in 500ml/17fl oz/2 cups water. I like to use the cooled water from boiling beetroots for this, as it adds extra colour and flavour and is full of goodness. It's a great way to make use of this if you have recently boiled a big batch of beetroots. Turn to the beetroot chapter for more about this. However, plain water does work just as well. Pour your prepared saltwater into the filled jar so that all of the turnips and beetroots are covered.

3   Place a weight on top to make sure the vegetables remain submerged. You can use a fermentation weight or a small clean glass jar filled with water. Do not secure the lid on your jar. Instead, cover with a dish towel or muslin/cheese cloth, so that air can filter but no debris, and use a rubber band to secure.

4   Place this on a shelf at room temperature, out of direct sunlight, and allow to ferment for around 1 week or until you are happy with the taste. The longer it is left to ferment, the sharper the taste. Once ready, store in the fridge for up to 3 months.

⚐ Skin

I never peel turnips. The skin is edible and an extra source of fibre and nutrients. What's more, they cook much better with the skin on. If you do peel your turnips, save the peelings to make into tasty crisps. Turn to page 214 for my guide to making crisps.

⚑ Leaves

Turnip tops are full of goodness. Use them as you would other greens, adding them to soups, stews and curries. The smaller young leaves are also good raw in salads. Try your turnip tops sautéed with olive oil, salt and garlic, or use them as an alternative to cabbage or other greens in a ramen (pages 53–5).

Mixed greens pesto: Turnip leaves can be used in place of traditional basil in pesto. Find my recipes on pages 67 and 158. You can use a mixture of greens to create a unique flavour, such as carrot tops, beet leaves, turnip leaves or spinach.

☑ My favourite ways to compleat:

Roasted turnips: Turnips have a milder taste when roasted and are great as a side or as an addition to your Sunday roast. Slice the turnips into even chunks, leaving the skin on, and reserve the leafy tops if you have them. Toss the turnips in a little rapeseed/ canola or olive oil and roast at 190°C/375°F/gas mark 5 for around 30 minutes, until softened and roasted. Serve as is or add to a pan with the shredded leaves, a little oil and a squeeze of lemon juice. Sauté briefly over a medium heat to wilt the leaves and combine. Taste and season with sea salt.

Dahl with turnips: We often add sweet potato or squash to dahl, but next time try adding some cubed turnips and simmering for around 20 minutes. For my kale and chickpea dahl recipe, turn to page 146 and try incorporating your new favourite root vegetable, as well as wilting some of the chopped turnip leaves into the dish.

• **A note about veggie offcuts broth:** Turnip offcuts and ends, as well as some leaves from the tops, can be saved with other vegetables to make stock. However, because of turnips' strong taste, add these sparingly or they could overpower your broth (page 232).

Useful food waste reducing recipes

If you're keen to reduce waste further in your kitchen and learn how to pickle, preserve and make the most of your ingredients, try these simple, frugal recipes and techniques. These are referred to throughout the book, so whether it's a pickle, ferment, infusion, stock or homemade nut butter, this chapter is your guide.

♻ How to Sterilize Jars

I have a few Kilner-style jars which are great for fermenting kimchi or pickling large amounts. However, I also save and reuse lots of shop bought jars. They work just as well and are easy to sterilize and reseal. To do this, preheat the oven to 160°C/325°F/gas mark 3. Choose only jars with metal lids. Wash the jars and lids in hot soapy water and rinse with hot water. Do not dry them. Place onto a baking tray in the preheated oven. Place in the preheated oven for ten minutes. Carefully remove and immediately fill with your chutney or pickle, secure the lid and seal.

Homemade Veggie Offcuts Broth

I refer to this recipe throughout my book because it is so simple to prepare and makes use of a huge amount of otherwise wasted vegetable offcuts, ends and skins – capturing their nutrients, flavour and colour ready for you to add to other meals. You can use the broth in soups or as a stock for curries, stews, risotto or any dishes where you might normally use shop bought stock. The only difference is that homemade stock isn't as salty, so you might want to season your dish a bit more, but taste and see if it needs it. Once cooled, I store my broth in jars in the fridge and use it within a week. You could also freeze it in tubs or poured into an ice cube tray.

For ease, I have a reusable bag which we keep in the freezer to fill with vegetable offcuts. You could make your broth using fresh vegetables, but it's rare to have enough scraps in one go. Once every few weeks, I cook a new batch of broth using the frozen offcuts. This keeps us in a near-constant supply of stock, all made from things we might normally think of as food waste.

Prep 5 minutes **Cooking** 1 hour

- One packed freezer bag of vegetable offcuts (a frozen weight of roughly 300–500g /10½oz–1lb 2oz. The more the better!)

Great for making broth:
- Onion and garlic skins and ends (these make up most of mine!).
- Root vegetable peels and ends.
- Squash and pumpkin peels and ends.
- Leek root end and green tops.
- Handful of carrot tops, beet tops or similar.
- Bean and pea pods.
- Mushrooms can be added but are also great for making a broth by themselves.
- Hard herb stalks, like those from rosemary.
- Courgette/zucchini and aubergine/eggplant stalk ends (only a few).

Avoid these in your broth:

• Brassicas like sprouts, cabbages or kale can cause your broth to taste bitter so add these sparingly if at all.

• Any fruit offcuts, peels or cores.

• Too much of any vegetable with an especially distinctive taste, such as sweetcorn husks and cobs, artichoke leaves or asparagus ends. It's better to make a broth from solely these (see pages 15, 113 and 137) or just include a few.

• Lettuce, cucumber, tomatoes, avocado or anything we consider to be salad.

• Only use offcuts from fresh vegetables, nothing from a can.

• Fennel.

1   Place your vegetable offcuts (fresh or saved and frozen) in a large lidded saucepan with enough water to submerge everything and allow space for the vegetables to float and simmer around during cooking.

2   Bring the pan to the boil and simmer over a medium heat, with the lid on, for 45 minutes to one hour. This will fill your home with amazing aromas from the stock, which will turn a deep colour and take in all of the goodness and flavour from the vegetables. Once ready, you could add some seasoning, like salt or mixed herbs to taste. However, I prefer to use my broth as is and add seasoning at the time of cooking, if needed.

3   Remove from the heat and carefully strain the broth into a heatproof container or jug. Use a slotted spoon to squeeze the vegetables and release all of the liquids. The vegetables should now be composted.

4   Once cooled, transfer the broth to jars, tubs or an ice cube tray for chilling or freezing.

Easy Universal Pickling

This simple pickling recipe can be adapted to work for different vegetables – from beetroots and their stalks, to onion offcuts or the ends of carrots and cucumbers. With a little common sense, you can also reuse the liquid from shop bought or homemade pickled vegetables – look out for murky brine, mould or pickles going bad – as long as you store them in the fridge and only do so once or twice. Save and sterilize old jars to refill with pickles and more.

Prep 15 minutes, plus maturing time

You'll need:
- A 1 litre/1 quart jar (or two smaller jars)
- 1 tablespoon salt
- 80ml/2½fl oz/1/3 cup vinegar of your choice

- Enough vegetables to fill your jar, chopped into bitesize pieces
- Optional aromatics, such as peppercorns, garlic cloves, mustard seeds or chili

1 In a jug, dissolve the salt in 240ml/9fl oz/1 cup water and add the vinegar. Layer the vegetables in the jar and pour over the liquid. Add any aromatics and seal the jar. The flavour will strengthen over time, but you can test it after one hour. Store in the fridge and eat within one month, or sterilize and seal your jar to store in a cupboard for a few months. If you have lots more to pickle, this recipe is easily upscaled. The liquid should remain one part vinegar to three parts water, and adjust the salt accordingly.

Simple Spirit Infusions

It's surprisingly easy to infuse spirits with leftover fruit, herb offcuts and fruit peels. Try combinations like lemon and lime peel gin, strawberry fruit and leaves vodka, orange peel brandy and mint with cucumber ends gin. This is lovely to make as presents.

Prep 5 minutes, plus at least a week infusing

- Fruit, herbs or peels to infuse (a handful or more)

- Spirit of your choice, such as vodka, gin or brandy (start with a 35cl bottle)
- Sugar (optional)

1   Cut your herbs, fruit or peels into small pieces and place in a jar. A handful is a good amount to start with, but you can add as little or as much as you like. The more you add, the deeper flavour you will create. Pour over the alcohol – again, as much or as little as you have available. Seal the jar and leave for at least a week. The colours and flavours will gently infuse and deepen over time.

2   Test a little of the spirit and dissolve in a little optional sugar to taste. Once you're happy, strain out the fruit, peels or herbs and set aside. Decant the spirit into a glass bottle or store in the jar. The fruits, peels or herbs can then be disposed of in your food waste, but they will have absorbed some of the alcohol so can be tasty. Try adding them to cocktails or trifle, or eat them with plant-based ice cream.

Infused Olive Oil

Chillies, garlic and herbs can all be used to infuse olive oil. I have a huge rosemary plant in our garden, and this is a lovely way to capture the flavour when the herb needs pruning. Use the oil as a dressing for salads, pastas and other dishes.

Prep 5 minutes **Cooking** 5 minutes

- Olive oil
- Aromatics or herbs for infusing

Suggested infusions
- 2 sliced whole fresh chillies (including seeds), peppercorns and

  a sliced garlic clove
- Sage or rosemary sprigs with a sliced garlic clove
- 2 sliced shallots and garlic cloves
- A few sundried tomatoes
- Orange or lemon peels
- Bunch of wild garlic and/or basil

1 Place your chosen aromatics or herbs in a saucepan with enough olive oil to fill a small jar or bottle. Warm over a medium to low heat for a few minutes to steep the flavours into the oil. You do not want this to boil or fry the ingredients!

2 Remove from the heat and carefully decant the aromatics or herbs into your jar or glass bottle. Using a funnel, carefully pour the oil into the container.

3 Once cooled, seal the container and store at room temperature for around a month or in the fridge for a few months. The flavours will continue to deepen over time.

• **Basil and soft herbs:** Basil, wild garlic, parsley or other soft green herbs should be blitzed in a food processor. You can use the stalks and leaves. Pour the oil into the food processor at room temperature and blend until everything is combined. Decant into a bottle or jar, store in the fridge and use within one week.

No Waste Nut and Seed Butters

I started making my own peanut butter to avoid the palm oil in shopbought nut butters. Palm oil production contributes hugely to deforestation and has horrendous impacts on wildlife and communities. Often palm oil is disguised in products and labelled as things like "vegetable oil", "sodium lauryl sulfate" or "palmate". Certified sustainable palm oil is a somewhat better option, but when it comes to nut butters, it is easy, fun and often cheaper to make your own. Follow the same steps to make a butter from any nuts or seeds, which can be bought packaging-free from zero waste shops. Also experiment with adding flavourings to your nut butters, such as maple syrup or cocoa.

Prep 30 minutes **Cooking** 15 minutes
Makes 1 large nut butter or 1 small seed butter

For nut butter
• 500g/1lb 2oz raw nuts
• 2 tablespoons oil of your choice
• 1 teaspoon salt, or to taste

For seed butter
- 100g/3½oz raw seeds, such as sunflower, pumpkin or squash
- 1 tablespoon oil of your choice
- 3 dates, or to taste
- ¼ teaspoon salt, or to taste

1   The process for making any nut or seed butter is very similar. First, preheat the oven to 180°C/350°F/gas mark 4. Then, place the nuts or seeds in an ovenproof dish and cook for 10–15 minutes until lightly toasted and fragrant. Remove from the oven and allow to cool a little.

2   In a food processor, blend the nuts or seeds with the oil for 10–15 minutes until smooth. Some food processors work quicker than others but be patient and take breaks if your processor feels hot. If you'd like some crunch to your nut butter, reserve 100g/3½oz nuts and add these at the very end and blend for 1 further minute. Once blended, taste the butter. I like to add salt to nut butters and salt and dates to seed butters. Add these to your taste or leave as is. Add any extra flavourings at this point, such as maple syrup. Decant into the jar and allow to cool. Store in the fridge and eat within a few months.

Homemade Granola with Oats, Nuts and Fruit

Like many packaged foods, most granolas you can buy contain palm oil. I prefer to make my own granola, fresh in the morning. It's much tastier, full of goodness and better value. Add chopped nuts and seeds of your choice, plus any other toppings, like dried fruit, toasted coconut chips (page 108) or cinnamony baked apple peels (page 12). Fresh fruit like apple and pear can also be diced and cooked with the granola. Delicious

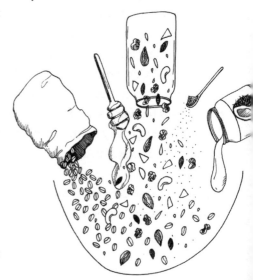

served warm with plant milk or yogurt. You can also pre-cook a big batch of granola and, once cooled, store it in a sealed jar in the cupboard for up to a week.

Prep 5 minutes **Cooking** 10 minutes
Serves 1

- 40g/1½oz rolled oats
- 2 tablespoons chopped mixed nuts
- 1 tablespoon seeds (pumpkin and/or sunflower)
- 1 tablespoon fruit or toppings (such as coconut chips, chopped apple, sultanas/golden raisins, raisins, dried fruit or apple/pear peels)
- 1 teaspoon milled flax seeds (optional)
- 1 teaspoon chia seeds
- 1 tablespoon sweetener (maple syrup, agave or golden/light corn syrup)
- ½ tablespoon melted coconut oil
- ¼ teaspoon ground cinnamon
- Plant milk or yogurt, to serve

1   Combine all of the ingredients in a bowl and mix well. Spread evenly on a baking tray and cook in the oven at 180°C/350°F/gas mark 4 for 7–10 minutes. Be sure to check on your granola frequently as this can quickly go from beautifully toasted to burned! Serve in a bowl, topped with plant milk or yogurt.

How to Grow Microgreens

Many people remember growing cress as a child but in recent years microgreens like this have risen in popularity. Effectively, microgreens are just leaves that are harvested when small – making them quick and easy to grow, as well as full of flavour. They are great for growing on a windowsill as a source of fresh goodness over winter or year-round if you don't have a garden. Enjoy them raw in salads or scattered over dishes. Compared to the mature produce, microgreens have been found to have a higher concentration of nutrients. What's more, because you can harvest and eat your microgreens fresh from the tray, they retain their nutrients as if they were direct from the field.

Try growing your own microgreens using seeds for produce like carrots, radishes, broccoli, beetroots, cabbage or rocket/arugula. You can use traditional growing seeds (great to use up any from an open packet) or buy seeds in bulk specifically for sprouting. Herbs, such as coriander/cilantro, basil, mustard and dill can also be sprouted from seeds for planting or any dried cooking seeds of these you may have. Dried pulses sold for cooking are also great, such as dried peas and beans to grow pea shoots (page 50). Soak these overnight before planting. Have fun experimenting with the different colours and flavours.

You'll need:
- A shallow tray, planter or reused produce container to sow into
- Compost
- Seeds

1 Fill your tray with a layer of moist compost then scatter in your seeds. Be generous with the seeds and sow thickly so that they are compact but not touching. Cover with a thin layer of moist compost and place on your windowsill.

2 Keep this moist and water carefully so that it does not dry out, but does not become too damp. Be careful not to damage any sprouting greens – they are micro after all!

3 Your greens should be ready to eat within a few weeks. Use scissors to harvest them. If you are careful, some will regrow, such as pea shoots, so leave a little of the stem and a leaf intact on these when harvesting.

Acknowledegments

Ever since I was a child, I've dreamed of one day writing a book, but it always felt like a bit of a fantasy. The idea for this book is a concept that kept coming back to me – a wild card at first that developed into a fully formed manuscript. Thank you to my editor Ella Chappell, for taking a chance on a debut author, working with me to hone my idea, believing in the book, and being so easy to work alongside. Thanks also to Daniel Culver and the rest of the brilliant team at Watkins and Nourish.

Thank you to my amazing partner, Nadia Davies, for supporting me through writing this book. You helped me create, taste and refine every recipe, you brought me cups of tea and banana bread, you listened to my rambles about chapters and were always there for a blustery walk at the end of the day. I couldn't have done it without you. Thanks to Bella, my dog, who is always sat by my side when I'm working. And to my mum, dad, sister and Katie.

I first started writing about sustainability thanks to the belief of my editor at *Psychologies* magazine. Thank you Suzy for encouraging me and for letting me write about topics that really matter. And to Lizzie, Vee, Lynne, Danielle, Leo, Emma, Nikki, Katherine and the many other fellow journalists and writers who have shared your words of wisdom and advice. My thanks also go to Frank Turner and The xx, whose music I listen to on repeat whilst writing.

My appreciation goes to Katy Beskow, Rose Elliot, Melissa Hemsley, Georgina Wilson-Powell and Bettina Campolucci Bordi who all kindly took the time to give me endorsements for the book. Thank you! Growing up as a vegetarian child in the 90s, Rose Elliot's cookbooks were a staple in our household, so her words are especially humbling.

A huge thank you to you, the reader, for supporting this book and taking a step into the weird and wonderfully waste-free world of compleating.

Index